"My Dearest Anna resonate with anyone who reads it. The letters provided are presented in such a way that you feel as though you are there reading over his shoulder as he writes to his beloved Anna. The story, written by Pvt. Moore's granddaughter, gives real insight into the mind and spirit of one man who fought for our country's freedom, while always keeping one thing close to his heart- his love."

   - AMY LAURIA
      (Minnesota Commemorative Air Force
      Wing Leader)

"Kara Martinelli captured the essence of what so many young men and women must have experienced during WWII. Her Grandfather's love and devotion for Anna is quite evident in the letters. I can almost picture him writing them as he trained for combat in the various bases around the country. Dick's writings are very descriptive which makes it easy for the reader to visualize the hardship and enthusiasm he shared for his country. I think readers will enjoy this "insiders" perspective and learn a little about history in the process."

   - BRAD LANG
      (CAF Red Tail Squadron Leader)

My Very Dearest Anna

MY GRANDPARENT'S LETTERS FROM WWII

KARA MARTINELLI

First Edition

Hemlock Films
www.hemlockfilms.com

Contact information:
info@hemlockfilms.com

Book Design by Kara Martinelli
Archival photos from personal collection and
US Air Force Museum Archives
Photography by Adam White

ISBN-10: 061556979X
ISBN-13: 978-0-615-56979-6

for my family

TRAVEL LIST

Nov. 27, 1943	New Philadelphia, OH to Cleveland, OH
Dec. 18, 1943	New Philadelphia, OH to Fort Hayes, Columbus, OH
Dec. 28, 1943	Keesler Army Air Field, Biloxi, MS
Feb. 14, 1944	Lubbock Army Air Field, Lubbock, TX
Apr. 28, 1944	Harlingen Army Air Field, Harlingen,TX
Aug. 17, 1944	Lincoln Army Air Field, Lincoln, NE
Sept. 12, 1944	Casper Army Air Field, Casper, WY
Dec. 28, 1944	Topeka Army Air Field, Topeka, KS
Dec. 8, 1944	Langley Field, Hampton, VA
Apr. 1, 1945	Salinas Army Air Field, Salinas, CA
May 2,1945	Mather Field, Sacremento, CA
May 8, 1945	John Rogers Field, Oahu, HI
May 9, 1945	Visited Honolulu, HI
May 10, 1945	Refueled at Palmyra Island then to Canton Island
May 11, 1945	Tarawa Island
May 12, 1945	Los Negros Island
May 14, 1945	Biak
May 16, 1945	Nadzab, New Guinea
May 30, 1945	Refueled at Biak then to Morotai
May 31, 1945	Refueled at Zamboanga Field, Mindinao then to Mindoro
July 17, 1945	Floridablanca, Luzon
July 29, 1945	Truck ride through Zig-Zag Pass to Subic Bay
Aug. 6, 1945	Embarked on LST to Okinawa
Aug. 11, 1945	Dropped anchor on Okinawa
Dec. 1, 1945	Clark Field, Luzon then to Nielson Field, Luzon
Jan. 14, 1946	Manila then to Clark Field, Luzon
Jan. 16, 1946	Fort McKinley, Luzon
Jan. 29, 1946	Boarded USS John Land at Manila Harbor, Luzon
Feb. 16 1946	San Francisco Harbor then to Camp Stoneman, Pittsburgh, CA
Feb. 22, 1946	Camp Atterbury, IN
Feb. 26, 1946	New Philadelphia, OH

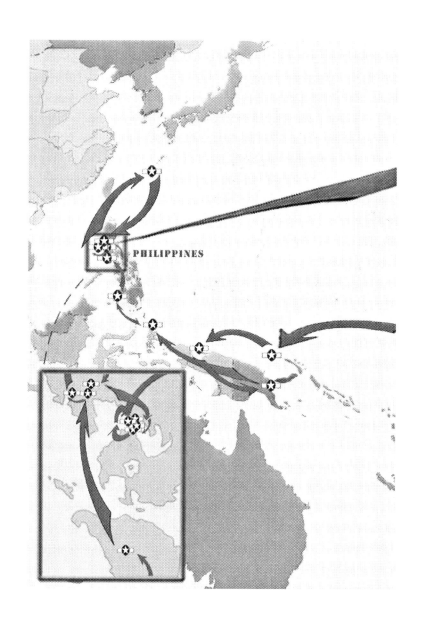

PHILIPPINES

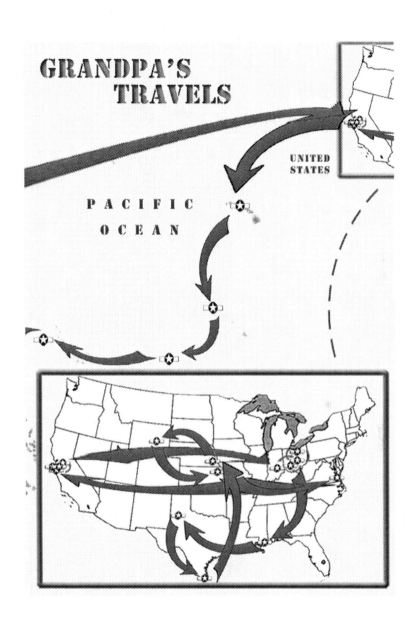

GRANDPA'S TRAVELS

UNITED STATES

PACIFIC OCEAN

INTRODUCTION

I grew up about a mile from my Grandparents house, so I spent lots of my time playing and hanging out there. My brother, two sisters, and four cousins were often there with me. We were all so close to them that they could be considered our second set of parents, as Grandparents are by definition. There was plenty of time spent with them working puzzles, playing video games, playing outside, and as we got older, sitting around the kitchen table just to talk and visit. It was so much fun to go to their house that they made it hard to stay away.

As I got older we would sit around the kitchen table more and more, and one of the stories that my Grandpa used to tell was the story of how he first met my Grandma. I didn't start to hear this story until after she had passed away in 1995 when I was 15. It wasn't until I was 18 that I realized that my Grandpa had been in World War II. I know he had said it at different moments throughout my youth, but I was just a kid, so I didn't *really* hear it. When he taught us to play poker he said "we used to play this in the Army, that's where I really learned how to play". Or when I was studying WWII history in high school, and he would make some familiar comment about whatever he was looking at in my textbook. But I was so wrapped up in just getting my homework done and getting the chance to play Nintendo, that I really wasn't absorbing what he was actually saying to me.

It was around the time when I was starting college that Grandpa got out his photo album to show me his pictures from the war.

I suppose I had probably said something that made him think about his time in the Air Corps. Prompting me to say something like "Grandpa, I didn't know you were in the war!" Which then lead to getting out his old album of photos. We would spend hours looking at all those pictures and he would tell me all the stories that would go with them. I learned all about his buddies and where he went and what he saw. It quickly became my favorite pastime with Grandpa. I was hooked. I couldn't get enough of his stories. It fascinated me to no end to hear whatever he could remember. I couldn't believe that my Grandpa had been a part of such a huge piece of history.

During my visits to Grandpa's house through the following years, I would sit in my usual seat at the small, round kitchen table, wedged between the window and the table, while Grandpa and I would chat. Mostly about the things I was up to and what he was doing around the house, but it would always lead to me asking to look at his scrapbooks again. Full of his photos and detailed notes and memories of his youth, that really wasn't that long ago. He was a part of history. A part of a *World* War. I was captivated by his stories. I still am, even though it has been years since we were last able to create new memories from Grandpa's old ones.

I'm not sure how many times we had gone through his photos, when he finally brought out his scrapbook of all the things he had collected during the war. Perhaps it took a while to show me because he had just assembled all of his stuff that he had saved, or maybe he had just remembered to retrieve it out of his incredibly organized attic (something else that I loved about his personality, he knew where everything was through his detailed notes and catalogues of his stuff). It contained things like old postcards, a Thanksgiving menu, government pamphlets about gonorrhea, and even his collection of short snorter bills. Short snorters were paper bills of the local currency that were glued together end to end that the men in the bomber crews would sign for luck. Then the owner of the short snorter would have to produce it upon request by the signer, and if they didn't have it on them then they were required to buy the signer a drink.

A few times our discussions lead to Grandpa getting out this purple box covered with a pattern of white flowers and would quietly open the lid and slide it across the table towards me. In it contained all the letters that Grandpa and Grandma had written to each other over the years while he was in the Army. And every time he would get them out, I would say something like, "this is amazing that you still have all these". I would never read the letters, I never wanted to. It felt too private. It was *their* history together, so I had no business reading them. They were given to me after Grandpa died in 2007. It took me 3 years after his death to even consider reading them. I was afraid to open them. Partly because I knew I'd lose the last of Grandpa's stories that I didn't know about. If I held on to them and didn't read them, I'd always have a piece of him waiting to have another one of our cherished conversations. I know sitting there with him all those days talking about the war and about Grandma made him so happy. And it made me so happy that I got to listen.

So I decided to finally open the box so that my family could share in all the details of their story. Which is really our story too. Our family's history. I wanted to make copies of the letters and put them into a book for everyone, so they could all have what I was so lucky to receive.

When I opened the box, I had to remove myself from whose handwriting it was that I was reading and whose story I was hearing. I had to, or I never would have made it past the first letter. If I stopped to think about my Grandpa writing to my Grandma, knowing how much he loved her and how many years he spent without her after her death, I knew I wouldn't be able to make it through just one letter without an onslaught of tears. And it was Grandpa, a voice I knew so well. One that I miss terribly.

On my first visit to the cemetery after Grandpa's death, I took one of the letters out of the box that Grandma had written. I read it to their unmarked graves. It was really rough just getting the words out through all the tears. And that was just one letter. So I knew this was going to be a difficult journey for me.

I tried to fill in the gaps as much as I remembered from our conversations. I haven't edited the letters because I didn't want to ruin the original text and risk taking something away from the history of the letters. So sometimes Grandpa and Grandma may be talking about people or events that aren't discussed any further or elaborated on. Which was part of the fun for me trying to figure out who and what they are talking about. Some people and events I never did figure out. Local events and their friend's history are discussed, but I can elaborate no furthur on who they were. It was like I was a detective trying to figure out the clues, and sometimes having to leave the mystery unsolved. The people with the answers are gone.

CHAPTER 1
Annie White Cabbage

When I first started asking questions about Grandpa's experience in the war, he couldn't wait to tell me the story of how he first laid eyes on Grandma. Even though this was years prior to when he left for the Army, he had to tell me right away. And it soon became the story I heard most often. Ask anyone in my family and they will probably tell you that they can't count the number of times they have heard it. I really do think it was his favorite story to tell. Not that we ever grew tired of it.

So the story of when my Grandpa met my Grandma goes like this. My Grandma Anna was in the 6th grade when she moved into my Grandpa Richard's neighborhood on the south side of New Philadelphia, Ohio. Grandpa was walking with his friend, Bob Alexander, when he noticed Anna and asked who she was. His friend responded, "Oh, that's just Annie Whitecabbage". Turns out that her real name was Anna Woytovich and the kid couldn't say her last name. Her family did shorten their name to Wyatt, so people would have an easier time pronouncing it.

Like clockwork, the story would always end with him grabbing my hand with tears coming to his eyes, saying simply "And I knew…" Which was followed by the same hand slap on the table that we all knew so well, as if giving the official signal to signify the end of the story. Though, I think secretly it was his way of changing the subject so he wouldn't be sad anymore.

He would have to spend several years waiting for his moment. Mostly because he never had the nerve to ask her out until he was leaving for the Army. And there was also the thing about Grandma dating Grandpa's cousin, Henry. I was told Grandpa never cared much for him in the first place, let alone he happened to date the girl he liked. This is another story I heard plenty about since one of the photos in his album was of Grandma and Henry together wearing sombreros.

After more than sixty years later, we were looking through the photos to use for Grandpa's funeral and there was that photo that I knew so well, with Henry cut out of it. So all that remains of it is just a half of a photo, of Grandma wearing a sombrero. I laughed so hard when I saw it, because I had seen that photo a few months prior and it was still in one piece. I don't know why Grandpa finally cut it in half, but it was very funny how much it still bothered him.

We'll never know what prompted him after all those years to cut him out, but I know the ultimate reason why. It just took him over sixty years to do it.

Grandma in her sombrero, sans Henry.

While Hitler's troops were rolling over Europe and North Africa, Japanese armies were invading China and South Pacific Islands. Unleashing horrors upon innocent people in the name of world domination.

After the Japanese attacked Pearl Harbor, the United States entered into World War II to protect our way of life and to help liberate those who had fallen under the Axis occupation. The country rallied to produce one of the largest war efforts in history. Young men volunteered to join the Armed Forces, while others were drafted. Women went to work in factories and took military jobs. Everyone collected their used cooking grease and metals to be used for munitions. They rationed gas and groceries. Factories now were producing airplanes, weapons, and military vehicles. They all wanted to do their part. And they did, turning America into a war machine. The nation was in full support to help our boys win the war and come home quickly.

Grandpa wanted to do his part too.

Grandpa would tell me that when he was young he had always loved planes and wanted to fly. While Grandpa was trying to join the Army Air Corps, he went to the doctor for his qualifying physical exam. The doctor told him that he was colorblind and he wouldn't be able to join the Air Corps, something that would make him ineligible. But someone told him about a doctor in town that didn't believe in color blindness. So Grandpa went to see this doctor, and at the end of the exam he said that Grandpa was fine and, most importantly, signed his slip saying that he was fit to join the Air Corps. And off my Grandpa went to fulfill his dream of flying into the wild blue yonder.

Grandpa had turned eighteen and was shipping off to the army when he finally got around to asking Grandma out on a date. They had promised to write each other, and they wrote for two years while he was away, and then got married shortly after his return.

The United States had been fighting in World War II for two years when Grandpa was inducted into the army in Cleveland, OH on Nov. 27th, 1943.

He then went back to New Philadelphia for a three-week induction furlough. On Dec. 18th he left for the Reception Center at Fort Hayes, in Columbus, Ohio. There he was assigned to the Air Corps for cadet training. Ten days later, on Dec. 28th, he was off to Keesler Army Air Field in Biloxi, Mississippi to report for basic training. He was assigned to the 58th Training Group, Class 140. While he was there he also took his classification tests for cadet training.

The following letters are all that remain of Grandpa and Grandma's courtship. I know most of Grandma's letters are gone, since Grandpa couldn't keep all of them throughout his time traveling in the Air Corps. I'm not sure what happened to the other missing letters, but I do know that they had made an unbroken promise to write to each other until he returned from the war.

CHAPTER 2
Keesler Army Air Field, Mississippi

Pvt. Richard B. Moore
A.S.N. 35922674
58*th* Trng. Grp. Class 140
Keesler Field
Mississippi

> Miss Anna Wyatt
> 208 St. Clair Ave. S.W.
> New Philadelphia
> Ohio

Jan. 8, 1944
12:00 P.M.

My Very Dearest Anna:
I'm starting this now but I won't have time to finish it till later today. I'm on detail today and have to be back in about 15 minutes. We're cleaning up an old building and it shouldn't take much longer.

I did take time off to go to mail call, naturally, and I'm mighty happy right now. I don't even mind working on the detail for this lucky boy. I had a letter from you. A nice long letter. That's all I needed to boost my morale. Maybe

I'll be lucky enough to hear from you this afternoon, or that may be too much to hope for. It still takes three days for a letter to get here and that's far too long.

I had better go now darling, but hang on, I'll be back. Till then don't forget – I love you.

4:00 P.M.

Here I am again, sweet, a little later than I expected, but I'm even in a better mood than usual for I stopped for the afternoon mail and had another wonderful letter from you. I'm awfully glad the mails starting to come through for I couldn't have stood one more day without a letter from you. This afternoon's letter only took two days. I guess if they had a mail call yesterday I would have gotten this morning's letter then. It was worth waiting for though. I'll read holes through both of them before tomorrow.

Your mother didn't have much of a vacation, did she? I was surprised to see her there too when I come down in the afternoon. You're beginning to think you have a swell Mom. I know you have. I like her and your Dad a lot. I never did get to really know them till this furlough and I think they're both pretty swell.

Anytime I go into a restaurant or cafeteria anymore all I can think of is a hamburger and coffee, then wish it was the Quaker and that you were sitting across the table instead of one of the crew. I didn't see "It Had to Be You" on the juke box or you can be sure it would have been played.

There's only one thing to keep this furlough from being perfect, it wasn't long enough. I could have stayed home much longer. In all other respects it was perfect. No wonder, anytime I'm with you is perfect.

Thanks for the name card, Anna. There's nothing wrong with it, it looks good with your full name on it.

What's wrong with that Weston Studio? Tell them that shelf of mine looks pretty bare and I can't wait much longer for your picture to put there. I'll have to get another furlough just to come home and get them on the ball.

I'm not writing because I made a New Year's resolution to that effect. It's the only chance I get to tell you I love you and I really want to write you. I doubt if I'll be able to keep that New Year's resolution even for some days it's impossible to find time. Up to now I haven't had any trouble, but I'll write every chance I get. Maybe if I miss one day I'll write the next. I hope you answer all of them. You'll hear from me often, honey, I promise that.

They don't have mail call on Sunday here, either, that's why yesterday was such a long day. So on Monday morning I get to the mailroom just as fast as I can.

So you don't believe that I enjoyed those two letters waiting when I got here. I did enjoy reading them and I'm not saying it just to be nice. If I got a letter from you a year old I'd enjoy reading it. I'm glad you're beginning to realize I love you. There are no maybes about it. I do, believe me, I haven't been telling you that all this time just because there's nothing better to do. If you don't think I love you, I'll just have to keep telling you until you know it.

Yes, I wish I went to New York. In a pig's foot I do. I wouldn't have had any fun in New York. All I would have done is sit around and wish I were home with you. I had a grand time at home darling, even being assistant hat check girl was a lot of fun. Mostly because I was with you. If I weren't such a drip and knew how to dance, we could have had a much better time.

How is my fellow assistant, Red? Has he recuperated yet? I believe he did most of the work between the two of us. I sat down most of the time, and most of my time was spent watching you get so mad that you broke your first resolution. I like Red, he seems like a pretty swell fellow.

9

*No, I'm not glad to be out of school. In fact, I'd give a
lot to be a senior right now. If I were going to school with
you, I'd enjoy it very much. I'll take exams in preference to
K.P. anytime. They never did bother me. If I remember
correctly we didn't have any exams at the end of the year
as seniors. So when you finish these semester exams your
worries will be over. If I were going to school now you'd
let me carry your books home wouldn't you. I didn't get to
walk home with anyone those last couple years, I'd have to
hop right on that old bike and hurry to Beatly's. It used to
make me so darned mad, yet I couldn't quit for he couldn't
find any one else to work for him and I hated to have him
stranded.*

*I still have to wonder whether or not we'd be going
together if I hadn't went to the Army. I think we would for
as much as I loved you, I couldn't have kept it to myself for
long.*

*I'm glad you don't get tired of my hanging around. I
like the thought of being with you the rest of my life. I'd like
nothing better. If you feel the same as I do, sweet, maybe
we will be together the rest of our lives, that is, after the
war's over.*

*I hope you don't think I waited till suppertime to come
down just for an excuse to go home. You know that's not so
for think of the time you had getting rid of me at night. I
hardly got out of bed before dinner time, then I'd have to
go see Ma or go up town for something and by the time I
made the rounds, it was around four o'clock. Then I headed
for your house. You didn't mean that did you? For it's not
so, for I can't remember a single time that I enjoyed saying
good night or good-bye to you, even if it was only for a
couple hours. Every hour with you seemed but about five
minutes, and I went to see you every possible minute I
could.*

10

I heartily agree with you about the furlough being too short, but we both know I've been pretty lucky in regard to furloughs. Many fellows have been in longer than I without getting home. I'm not complaining, I guess praying does do some good after all. One of these days I'll break down and start going to church. I should have started long ago.

I really surprised everyone when I come home this time, including myself. When we walked in the Colonel's office and he started raising hell I could see that furlough flying out the window. I still couldn't believe it till I was walking down the good old streets of Phila.

Someone said Red Skelton is here on the field in person and is giving a show tonight. I'll have to see him if he is. I missed Gary Cooper at Casper. After all you don't get a chance every day to see a celebrity.

I went to the show last night. It was "Guest in the House" with Anne Baxter. I didn't like it too well. It was probably because you weren't there beside me. I'll never be able to enjoy a show anymore unless you're with me.

Your ring feels like it was made for me. I'll bet you had to use a ball of sting on mine. I imagine it would be rather clumsy. I should have got it for my little finger in the first place then it would fit you. I'm glad we traded rings. I'll never be without it, ever. You know, a lot of guys who fly have something like a ring from someone they love and would never fly without it. You can bet Ill never fly or be without that ring for a minute. I hope that in the near future you'll be wearing a different kind of ring. I feel pretty darned proud to be able to wear your ring, and not someone else.

I think I saw that article in the Digest about the same time you did so you needn't bother sending the questions. I've already answered them and I also am very much in love. I can answer nine of them yes, and the other I'm not sure about. Most of them I'd go farther than yes – I'd say

11

absolutely, positively yes. If Doe Adams knows what he's talking about I'm head over heels in love. I don't need a doctor to know that though. It just confirms what I've always known.

I guess I'd better close for now, honey. If you aren't bored stiff by now, you have nerves of steel. I guess once I get started on the subject of loving you, I can't stop. I do love you darling, terribly. If you don't realize it by now, you never will. So till tomorrow, good night and keep those wonderful letters coming.

Love forever and ever,
Dick

In this letter Grandpa mentions going to church in the future. When I read this, I was surprised, for Grandpa never did care much for organized religion. I have heard stories about a lot of the men that came out of WWII had given up on God and religion. I never really knew fully what Grandpa believed in or why he believed it or even when he started believing it. I just know that before he died, he told me he didn't believe in God and that he didn't want any sort of funeral. He said he didn't like having one for Grandma and didn't want to have one for himself either.

Jan. 30, 1944

Dear Anna:

I got two letters from you and a box from home so I did better than usual today. When I got that box I suddenly became very popular and had more friends than I knew I had. I still have some stuff left though.

It's sort of a coincidence for Ade and Ray to meet again so far from there. Maybe I can meet some of the guys sometime.

I'm having a harder time than anyone keeping up with that cousin of mine. I got one letter from Gene in N. Carolina and he said he was going to Indiana.

I've heard "Russian Winter" but none of the others. They have juke boxes in the P.X.'s and I catch up on them a little.

You're like me, I always brought books home but never opened them. I always found something else I wanted to do more than homework.

How do you look as a tangerine? Don't stay that way. You were much nicer looking as you were.

The other R. Moore doesn't get my mail. He hardly ever gets any mail at all. Maybe he should get some so he'd feel better. If I got as little mail as him I'd head over the hill. I'm getting plenty of mail. I'm having a hard time keeping it answered. I only answer the most important first. And yours heads the list of importance.

What new girl do you mean that is working at Holton's?

Today was one of the warmest I've seen for a long time. It was like a summer day at home.

Did anyone I know go on the last trip? I heard about Hayes too. I wonder where they'll send them.

I didn't know it was such a big secret that the soldier was writing to Dort.* I thought sure she'd tell you.

I never knew how to make a bed either till I got in the Army. Say, if you learn all that stuff, you can do all the

13

work. Have they still got home economics? Learn to cook. Or can you? I think you're just modest.

I run across Roy again tonight. Him and his buddies were going to get something to eat.

You can tell people you're seventeen and that way even it up again. What about Paul? Has he left yet?

We still can't send clothes to the laundry. I was going to wash some today but it was so nice I went to the show.

"A Guy Named Joe" was on. Has it been there yet? I liked it a lot. Spencer Tracy played in it. It was about the Air Corps too. That's not the reason I liked it.

You should see the line-up for shows. There's a full house every time and the line goes for two blocks or more. That's a double line. You look at the line and wonder how all of them get in.

Tomorrow's pay day. Let's go out tomorrow night. I may be just kidding there but when I get home I'll mean it. I'll go right to the P.X. and get a couple cokes and get plastered. That's a funny thing. They don't care how drunk a guy gets here so long as they don't disturb anyone or raise the devil. When I was on guard duty in quarantine I seen them carry guys in and nothing was said. They have to get it in Biloxi though. Don't worry, I don't intend on getting drunk or I don't even care if I never get to Biloxi. Roy says there's nothing to do once you get there and if Roy can't find something to do nobody can.

There's a rumor that the washout list will come out tomorrow. I hope so cause I'm anxious to know if I made it or not. I'm afraid I'm in for a big let down but I want more than ever to pass.

I made the rounds today. I believe I was in every P.X. in camp. It's the first day we've had off for a while so I put on my O.D.'s and took a walk. I come in tonight to catch up on some writing.

I'll close now. Goodnight. Don't look now, but I think you're wonderful.

Love
Dick

*My Grandma was a good friend with Grandpa's sister Dorothy. In her letters, my Grandma refers to her as Dort.

AIR CORPS TECHNICAL SCHOOL
Keesler Field, Mississippi

Feb. 8, 1944

Dearest Anna:
I am very, very happy. If you were here I'd give you a kiss. I don't know if it was your praying or what but I do know I made it.

I took the test today to see how much college I'll need. They'll probably say send that dope back to grade school. I hope I get sent to a college close to home. Then maybe I'll see you before I had even hoped.

They're shipping them out pretty quick now so with luck I'll be out of here within a month.

We have K.P. tomorrow. It's the first for about three weeks so I can't kick. I feel too good to care anyhow.

I went to the show last night. When I come back, the guys said my name had been called on a list of fellows. I was worrying whether it was washouts or not. I found out this morning.

15

I'll have to get to bed because we have to get up at 2 for K.P. and I need the sleep. Sorry it's so short but I'll write more next time. So long and thanks again for the prayer. That did it.

Dick

P.S. That's not the only reason I'd like to kiss you.

CHAPTER 3
Lubbock Army Air Field, Texas
On-the-Line Training

On Feb. 14th, 1944, Grandpa reported to Lubbock Army Air Field for On-the-Line Training as a part of the Cadet program.

Pvt. Richard B. Moore
A.S.N. 35922674
On-the-Line Trainee- 7th Increment
495th T.E.F.T.S.
Lubbock Army Air Field
Lubbock, Texas

> *Miss Anna Wyatt*
> *208 St. Clair Ave. S.W.*
> *New Philadelphia*
> *Ohio*

Lubbock Army Flying School
LUBBOCK, TEXAS

Feb. 14, 1944

Feb. 14, 1944

Dear Anna:

Here's those songs I promised you. I don't need them anymore so instead of copies here is the book. Now you can sing your head off.

This field's paradise. Pork chops for supper. Delicious, big pork chops, bread with jelly, apple pie. I'm telling you, I don't believe it. They must like us in this army. No wonder the guys stationed here don't want to leave.

I went over to the show tonight. "Madam Curie" was on. It wasn't bad. Maybe you saw it.

I'll write again tomorrow and tell you more. Till then.

Love,
Dick

Lubbock Army Flying School
LUBBOCK, TEXAS

Feb. 16, 1944

Dear Anna:

Yesterday I went out on the line. In the morning we just sat around in a building. Then they assigned us to crew chiefs. They have two kinds of planes here, Curtiss AT-9 and Cessna AT-17. The AT-9 is all metal and that is the one I was put on. We had to wash them off with gasoline and shine them up. They haven't been cleaned for a year and they sure are dirty. We'll be cleaning them for a week. Then we'll learn how to gas them, put in oil and a few other things like that. Then we'll learn to taxi them around the field.

One fellow caught one on fire yesterday. They were learning to taxi them already. He forgot to turn a switch and when it started the engine caught fire. They got it out

18

right away though and nothing was hurt. I think I'll like it here. Even washing them is fun. At least I know I'm in the Air Corps now and not in the infantry.

The sergeant said he'd try to get us a ride in them before we leave. I hope so.

We are supposed to be here 30 days. Then we go to college. I hope. We were supposed to go to college from Keesler, but they drug this line business out and here I am. I hope they don't find anything else.

Some think we'll go right to pre-flight from here but I doubt it. I'll need more mathematics and physics before I can go there.

This is an advance training school for twin-engine flying. There's a class of cadets here now.

In a couple weeks they'll be graduating. They'll have their wings and commissions. I sure wish I was that far. I'll be plenty lucky to get through college even.

They're pretty swell fellows too. They aren't smart and cocky like you'd imagine. They really like flying too, they say there's nothing like it.

They keep us as busy here as they did at Keesler. We get up at 6. Eat at 6:15. Go out on the line at 7 till 10:30. Drill till 11:30. Eat. Go back on the line at 12:15 till 3:45. One hour physical training. Eat at 5:30 and we're through unless they have something else they want done.

It's really windy down here. And it's a cold wind too. The sun is out nice and bright but it's still chilly.

Another good thing here is K.P. It's a snap. They pick five guys out of the squadron. They have K.P. 3 days straight, but it's only for 8 hours a stretch instead of 16 or more like Keesler. They have permanent K.P.s here. Men who do nothing but work in the kitchen so the K.P.'s work here is short and easy, I haven't had it yet but I probably will before I leave. But with all the time off you have with the job, it will be O.K.

19

I sure miss the mail. I had a letter from you the day we left Keesler. I don't suppose I'll get any mail till next week yet. That will be a very happy day, believe me.

We're quarantined here for two weeks again. But here it's a laugh. It just means we can't leave the post. After two weeks we're eligible for passes to town. I don't suppose there's much in this town either but I may go in to see what it's like. I suppose it's like Dalhart, but I don't know exactly what Dalhart's like, just what Gene told me.

The planes around here are thicker than flies. They're flying around all the time and a dozen of them around at a time. I thought that at advanced they learned to do some fancy flying, but I guess they get that after they have their wings.

I can't think of anything else. I suppose you're bored by now, cause you don't care about planes, but there's not much more to tell about.

So long and write soon. The only thing I miss more than your letters is yourself so keep them mail clerks here busy.

Love,

Dick

P.S. How do you like that address? It's a lulu, ain't it? If you write it on the front you won't have room for your address or the stamp. It takes as much time to write as a letter.

Feb. 18, 1944

Lubbock Army Flying School
LUBBOCK, TEXAS

Feb.18, 1944

Dear Anna:

Well I had a hard day's work today. We went out on the line this morning and waited around till 9:30 and they told us to go back and change our uniforms and go to the show. It was only a couple training films but it was O.K.

It's raining and cold. It's more like sleet. The ground's wet and icy. One of the fellows walked out the door on the top step hit the sidewalk in 1/10th a second flat. No kidding, he did a complete loop. He wasn't hurt so it was funny. Maybe it wasn't so funny to him, but he was laughing too.

When we went out this afternoon, they told us to go back and wait to go sign payroll. Everything was slippery this morning. We went out to pre-flight the planes or warm them up. The crew chief got hold of the handle to put his foot on the wing wall and started to go up to the cockpit. His foot slipped and down he come. His foot went through the fuselage and ripped a big hole in it. I'll put a piece of the fuselage in the envelope.

All I've been doing out on the line is watching them start up the engines and riding in them while they taxi, I know a little about starting them. The guy was going to show me this morning but they sent us back. There's about 2 dozen switches to throw and 50 instruments to watch. Maybe that's an exaggeration but it seems like it anyhow.

I'm really having fun now. This place is an example every army camp should follow. I've been to a show practically every night.

I seen "Standing Room Only" last night. It probably has been to Phila. It was really good. I laughed my head off.

In physical training yesterday we went over the obstacle course. That's a lulu. We have to climb walls, jump hurdles, crawl on our stomachs under a wire screen, hand walk across wood rungs, and swing across a ditch on ropes. It don't look tough but you're out of breath when you finish.

This will have to be short. There's nothing more to write about. I can't write here anyway, these guys are arguing about something and I can't concentrate.

Several of the fellows have mail already so I should get some by tomorrow. Here's hoping. I can't wait to hear from you.

Till next time.

Love,

Dick

*Included in the envelope of this letter was a small rectangle piece of silver fuselage from the crew chief who kicked a hole in the plane. It was still in there after all these years.

Lubbock Army Air Field, Feb. 1944.
Front Row: Richard B. Moore (Grandpa), Wally Kramer, Art Tlucka, Pete or Maurice Westfall.
Back Row: Bud Laino, Les Smith, Saviano, Chuck Leistner, and Jim Strachan.

Lubbock Army Air Field, Feb. 1944.
Front Row: Richard B. Moore (Grandpa), Bud Laino, Saviano
Back Row: Les Smith, Louis Perret, Wally Kramer, Ed Knill, Jim Strachan.

Lubbock Army Flying School
LUBBOCK, TEXAS

Feb. 20, 1944

Dearest Anna:
Today is Sunday and we have the day off. I slept practically all morning. I felt in a mood to write letters so here I am again, I still haven't got any mail here. It surely should be coming tomorrow, from home if not Keesler.
Last night they had a P.R.C. picture at the show. That was more like home than anything I've done yet, it was a double feature, The Andrews Sisters in "Swingtime Johnny" and Buster Crabbe in "Nabonga". The last was the P.R.C. It was about a gorilla and it stunk. It was just

23

like the double features back home at the Union on Saturday night. The only thing missing was you. We could have really made fun of that one.

For the last couple days we have done absolutely nothing. But the weather has cleared up today, so I suppose there will be plenty to do tomorrow.

The college in Lubbock is Texas Tech and they are graduating a class of cadets in a couple weeks so we figure that's where they intend on sending us. I guess the college isn't very nice, so I hope we don't go there. I'm perfectly satisfied here.

My name will come up for K.P. in the next couple of days. I guess it's pretty easy K.P. so I don't mind it. This is about the only place I've heard of where guys want on K.P. That shows you how screwy the place is.

"Jane Eyre" is on at the show today. The fellows that seen it say it's good so I'll have to go tonight. I've never seen so many shows since I've been in the army.

I'm writing this in the day room. It's nice. There's a good radio at one end, a pretty varnished floor, lots of soft chairs, good writing tables, magazines, a pool table, card tables. It's a swell setup.

The service club is nice too. It has a lot of writing tables. It has a radio, a juke box, and a phonograph with all the latest records. I heard that "Honey Song" and I don't know what you meant about the words. Maybe I heard the wrong one or something.

Have you heard "Mairzy Doats"? That's a screwy song. It's sort of cute though. I heard guys singing it and didn't catch on to it till I heard the whole song.

I can't think of anything else to write about so I'll quit for now. When I get mail I'll do better and write more. I just don't know what to write about. So long. Keep writing.

Lots of Love

Dick

Dear Anna:

It isn't such a bright sun shining day here. Yesterday it was until evening, then the wind started blowing and it got colder than the devil. It's still chilly this morning, but the wind's gone. We'll be pulling out anytime now so I may be getting some of the northern weather before long. We expect to leave in the next couple of days. And it's still Michigan.

No, I don't go to church. I went once at Fort Hayes and never went since. They don't make you go. About the only way they could is threaten us with extra work but they don't seem to care whether we go or not.

I didn't even know Jean Willis knew Toad. Who is her boyfriend?

If the map don't have Philly on it's no good. You should throw it away or something.

I've often thought of calling up but I wouldn't know where to call or anything so I never did. It takes too long too. Some fellows call to Cleveland and it takes three or four hours to get the call through.

It's a lot of trouble moving all right. The only thing is we don't have all the furniture to move.

There's a good show on here today. It's the "Purple Heart". It's about the American flyers killed by the Japs. I saw "Private Hargrove" the other day. It was darned good. It's not a whole lot like army life though. I seen "A Guy Named Joe" at Keesler. You can't join the Air Corps if you're over 26, but they don't kick you out of flying when you reach it. There's plenty of good flyers up in the late thirties. They're not fighter pilots but a lot of good bomber pilots.

I went skating once in Lubbock, but it was such a dinky little dump and no good at all for skating that I didn't have any fun. Tuscora is no first class rink but it has that place beat by a mile.

No I never heard from Ade at all. Maybe he never got my letter or something.

Well there's not much to write about so I might as well close for now. So long. I'll be seeing you (if I get up North, I will).

Love,
Dick

March 24, 1944

Dear Anna:

Well by now I should have been at Michigan State but here I am still at Lubbock. I'm not even sure if I'm still in cadet training. The announcement over the radio said 36,000 who had completed basic training and qualified for training as pilots, bombardiers, and navigators would be transferred to ground forces. And that just fitted us fellows here. There were a lot of fellows here felt pretty low. But now we're not sure if it includes us.

They would have probably told us if we were washed up but they haven't said anything yet. I'm hoping for the best though.

If I even get to Lansing I don't think I'll get home on a three day pass because as far as I know there's no such thing as a three day pass in college. There has been some colleges that give furloughs after you complete the course but that's not all the time. It's not very far though. I could probably make it home in half a day with a fast train. But why dream of such things as that. I doubt if I'll even get there now.

Yes, we have had some swell times together and I hope we'll have many more.

I had a dream about Judy last night. She was up in Pauline's front room and I walked in. She still knew me and said Dick.

It's just like spring down here. I haven't seen snow for so long, I'll forget what it looks like.

I'm back on the night shift again and the way they've arranged things we're on nights every other week. They've clamped down on us. This was the new system for the new trainees to come and since we stay they put it on us.

Well, there's no more news, so I'll close for now. So long till next time.

Love
Dick

Lubbock Army Flying School
LUBBOCK, TEXAS

March 30, 1944

Dear Anna:
Well today's my day off so I can get some writing done. I can't understand this mail situation. Mom said she hadn't heard from me for over a week, and I know I never went that long without writing to either her or you. Mine comes in regular anymore.

27

You can expect anything in the Army so it's no great surprise that we didn't go to Michigan.

I saw "Cover Girl" today. It's not too good but it's better than nothing at all. That Rita Hayworth. I didn't like her so well in a few pictures but this one she's all right.

Those C.A.P. guys act too much like they're already in. They act cockier than these cadets who are almost finished.

That "sir" business gets me too. You know you're supposed to say "sir" to an officer and half of the time out there when one of those flying officers asks me something I don't even say sir. You can get by with it with those fellows though, most of them are square guys. But it don't pay to forget it with the ground officers. If you'd forget it with our Major he'd blow his top.

That Philips guy is nothing but a flirt and you can tell him I said so. That's all he did when I was in his class.

You're not kidding, it's a lot worse to get up for work than school. I should be going to school right now. It'd be nice to be studying again right now.

There's always people who will steal, that's sure. You wouldn't think a soldier would be low enough to steal from another, but there's plenty who do it. And it goes on plenty right in this camp too.

Tommy and his girl will probably make up again. They usually do if they really like each other. I guess it's all up to the one's who break up whether they should give the gifts back. I couldn't say myself because I never want to be in that situation.

Phyliss is far too young to do as she does but if her family don't worry about it, I know I certainly don't care.

I think I'll make you pay my way. After all, the women are doing everything else the men use to so why not that (I'm only kidding). For instance, there's a WAC (Women's Army Corps) out here that drives the jeeps and gas trucks. She's really rough. I'll bet she can out cuss many a man. Then there's another who drives trucks and she's as quiet as can be. Some of these WACs are really characters.

Pete's lucky. If I was ever sent home and had to wait for a wire to go back to camp, I'd blow up the telegraph office.

If I can go through in the Air Corps I'd rather be in the Army than home but if they transfer us to some ground branch I think I would tell them to stick the Army you know where.

I don't know of anything else to write. I suppose you're bored stiff by now. I'll give your love to this Moore rat and if you'll please look up a girl named Anna give her <u>all my love</u>.

Dick

April 3, 1944

Lubbock Army Flying School
LUBBOCK, TEXAS

Dear Anna:

If you got a chance to take those Kent tests you should take them. That is if they still go to Kent, or did they quit sending them there? I had a lot of fun going even though I didn't do much good.

I think senior dues was a dollar. It's a lot of hooey but I guess if you want to go to any of the dances or parties you should pay it. I did and never went to them. I guess I missed out on a lot of fun but I'm not anymore.

Who the heck are the Rambling Rec's? I guess it's the Recreation Hall but I've never heard of it before.

*A guy in one of those cowboy hats back in Phila. looks
funny, but here a guy in any other kind of hat looks funny.
Practically every one of these Texans wears one of those
hats and cowboy boots. It's a wonder they don't pack
pistols.*

*I saw "Heavenly Body" with Hedy Lamarr last night
and I almost went to sleep in it. It was pretty funny in spots
but there wasn't much of a plot to it and it got pretty
boring.*

*It hasn't been much like Spring here either the last few
days. It rained a little yesterday and it warmed up today so
it's more like Spring this morning.*

*We start nights again tonight. We worked all day
yesterday but we'll be off again next Sunday.*

*It's beginning to look as though we'll be at Lubbock for
the duration. All these officers assure us that we're still in
but whether they're just saying that is beyond me.
Meanwhile they're closing down all the colleges. So if
we're still in I don't expect to go to college. We'll probably
go right into pre-flight, which will be a lot tougher without
college.*

*Don't worry about me not wanting to hear from you so
often. The only thing is it makes me feel bad cause I never
have time to answer them all and we have a lot less time
since we went on a new schedule. Practically everyday this
week we had to work the whole day. I'm way behind on all
my mail but I always answer yours first when I get the
chance to write.*

*So forgive me if I don't write as often and tell Anna that
this Moore kid still misses her.*

Love
Dick

Lubbock Army Flying School
LUBBOCK, TEXAS

April 7, 1944

Dear Anna:

Well, I guess I'm all washed up before I even get started. I've been expecting it but I was hoping pretty hard that it would never come. I'll still be in the Air Corp, maybe as a gunner, radioman or mechanic. I can't see gunnery so much but the others would be O.K. as long as I can't fly.

I was beginning to get my hopes up that I was still in, so it was sort of a blow. The Colonel talked to us and told us we were out. All those fellows who came from other branches will go back and the ones who were in the Air Corps remain although not as flyers.

Your cousin may not get in for a while. Those who enlisted when 17 and are not yet in won't go for a while.

"Cover Girl" wasn't too good a show. I saw a better one yesterday. It was "Up in Arms" with Danny Kaye and Dinah Shore. This is Kaye's first show and he's pretty good. He's sort of silly but he's still good.

I liked Rita Hayworth in the first picture I saw her in but lately she hasn't been so good, but this picture she was a lot better than usual.

Harold Maurer is a pretty nice guy. I don't think he'll be getting in the Air Corps for a good while though.

I went skating last night and had a lot more fun than before. It's a nicer rink than the one in town. This one's right on the edge of town. It's even a better rink than Tuscora. There wasn't many there either and that's when it's fun.

I'm on nights this week. We've been working pretty late too. We only had 8 planes on our line and 7 of them

31

couldn't fly at night. Then they changed the planes around and we got 14 that all fly at night. So we have more to do.

I'll put in a couple pictures. They're the same ones I sent Mom but you can always use them to chase the rats away.

I'll close for now, so long.

Lots of Love,

Dick

P.S. Thanks a million for that Easter card. It's wonderful. I'm sorry I couldn't find a nicer one to send you but the town was cleaned out of cards.

My heart breaks reading about his disappointment of not being allowed to be a pilot, since I know he was so fond of airplanes and probably dreamed about it since he was a kid. While he was in high school he sketched all of the warbirds, now kept in his infamous album, that apparently helped him ace his airplane spotting exam. But he never seemed sad about what he got to do, and following the war, the B-24 became his favorite plane.

April 21,1944

Dear Anna:

It sort of looks as though I'll be taking another train ride in the next few days. Couple days would be more exact. But as the saying goes, once you get in Texas you

32

never get out and I believe we're going to Harlington. It's down near the Mexican border, as far south as you can go, right on the toe of Texas.

It's a gunnery school, so even though I never got the chance to fly them I may get the chance to fly in them. I don't think Mom and Dad will like the idea, and I don't like it exceptionally well, although I don't actually dislike the idea. I know darn well Gib won't like it. He was against me trying to fly in the first place, and when it comes to gunnery - well - I know what he thought of it when Gene had ideas of being a gunner. But I have no choice in the matter. So a gunner I'll be. They haven't told us positively it would be gunnery but that's the only thing I know they'd give a physical for and we had a physical today.

They rejected those over 6 feet and a gunner can't be over that so it looks like a sure thing.

I come into town tonight for a last look. I'm writing this at the U.S.O. as you can see by the paper.

Today's a big day in Texas. It's San Jacinto day celebrating Texas' independence from Mexico. Even the banks close. It's sort of Texas state national holiday. They're having a big dance here tonight. I'll be they're having twice as big a time in Mexico. They're so glad they got rid of it. I don't suppose they fought too hard to keep it anyway. You know this war's being fought because we tried to give Texas to Germany and Japan. You see how hard they're fighting so they won't be stuck with it.

Well I'll close for now. So long and keep writing for the way the Army works we're liable to still be here.

Lots of Love,
Dick

I remember Grandpa telling me the story of how he was short that they had made him a tail gunner. Getting in and out of the gunner positions was very tight in the small spaces of the aircraft, so the Air Corps would have the shorter guys become gunners. I've had the oppurtunity to route around on a B-24 a handfull of times through the years and they are very close quarters. It must have been really uncomfortable to ride in it for those long flights that they took. I can see why they would recruit shorter people for those positions, if they were any bigger, they wouldn't fit.

On April 28th, 1944, Grandpa left Lubbock for the Army Gunnery School in Harlingen, Texas. He reported to Harlingen Field for training as an aerial gunner.

He was granted a furlough from May 15th to May 27th, which explains the time where no letters were written, since he was home with Grandma enjoying the little time that they had together.

CHAPTER 4
Harlingen Army Air Field, Texas
Gunnery School

Pvt. Richard B. Moore
A.S.N. 35922674
Section 1
2123rd AAF Base Unit
H.A.A.F.
Harlingen, Texas

Miss Anna Wyatt
208 St. Clair Ave. S.W.
New Philadelphia
Ohio

May 29, 1944
6:00 P.M

Dearest Anna:
    I went over to mail call tonight and got my mail. There
was two letters there from you. I didn't tear them up though
like you said. I've even read them over a couple times. I

hope I have some more tomorrow. Even if you don't feel like writing this summer I hope you feel like it long enough to write to me, because your letters mean everything to me.

Why are you always knocking your spelling? I've very seldom seen a misspelled word in your letters. I probably miss more than you do.

So you're figuring on being a secretary. I hope not for long, for I have other plans, Miss Wyatt. I have another occupation all picked out for you. I hope you know what I mean.

I know darned well I missed most of the show when I was with you. It's a good thing I had already seen most of it then, for it didn't make any difference.

I don't think Tommy was kidding about getting paid. I have two months coming. We signed the payroll as soon as we got in last night. But that was only for one month and we get paid the second, so you can expect that pin soon after. Mom already got my bond for April but I haven't got my money. I guess that's life though.

Once I get started in gunnery I'll get flying pay and that adds up to a good bit. If I ever make Corporal and get flying pay I'll be making $100 a month. Twice what I get now. And if I make it through gunnery I have a good chance of getting Corporal or Sergeant before going across. Wouldn't you feel proud to address your letters Sgt. Moore? There I go again dreaming but you said it didn't hurt to dream and they sometimes come true.

Maybe it was your hoping that helped me out though. It seems that every time you back me up on something it turns out all right for me, with you behind me I can't miss.

You know what, I run across my ration book when I unpacked my stuff and with the few stamps there were in there, you were operating a black market. But if all black markets were as good as that, well there wouldn't be any complaint. I won't tell the O.P.A. as long as you don't have any other customers but me. You're a very precious commodity and I want you all to myself. (Selfish, aren't I?)

We were on work detail this morning and afternoon. Tomorrow it's K.P., but I don't go on unless one of those on the list gets sick. I'm now peddling vitamin pills so all the boys will be hale and hearty tomorrow.

This field has changed quite a bit since I left. The chow seems better. I thought it would taste awful after that good home cooking but I was greatly surprised because it was good.

And these permanent party guys don't seem to be such rats anymore. I think I can get to like this place if I try hard enough.

I think I'll be starting training this Saturday maybe or next Saturday for sure. I sure hope so for I'm mighty anxious to get started.

I think I'll get cleaned up now and go over to the show. "Show Business" is on. I think it's another of those musicals with a lot of stars. I sure wish you were here to go with me.

I don't know how the mails going to come in now. One fellow went home on furlough and when he got there the house was empty. His folks had moved to Chicago. So he lost a whole day of his furlough getting there. They had been writing him two whole weeks before he left telling him they were going to move but through someone's bungling here at the post office he didn't get his mail and he just lost out there. I wish they had someone handling the mail who knew what they're doing.

I guess I've run down now. You should be getting pretty bored by now so I'll finish up.

But there's one thing I must tell you Anna. I love you very much and the happiest day of my life will be when I can come home to stay and be with you always. So long and write soon.

Love
Dick

Darling Anna:

I'm writing pretty late tonight but it's not my fault. I just got off K.P. They couldn't find one fellow and since I was first on the list of extras I was picked to take his place. I'd like to find that guy right now, oh what I could do to him. If he would have been on, as he should I would have just laid around the barracks to be on hand in case they needed an extra K.P. And they wouldn't have needed any so I would have had a wonderful day.

I had a fairly easy job though, working in the dining room serving the food. The only thing wrong was they decided to take inventory of equipment and we had to stack every tray, knife, fork, spoon, pot, pan, pitcher, etc. in the whole mess hall in neat piles to be counted. So instead of getting done at 7 it was 8:30 when we finished.

There was another bunch of cadets come in yesterday and I heard more come in today so it may be longer than I expected till we start. So it means more K.P. and details. What a life. What's Hargrove got that I haven't.

One fellow sneaked out and got some of our mail for us, so I got your letter. But the funny part is we had a pretty good Sergeant and he had a fellow go after the mail so I

38

would have gotten it anyway. I was expecting a letter from you, so if no one would have gotten the mail, I believe I would have gone after it myself.

If I don't keep you busy answering my letters, just what will you do to me? Don't forget the next time I come home I may be a gunner and I'll bring a .50 calibre with me to protect myself. But I'll do my best to keep your mailbox filled and then there'll be no reason to protect myself.

I would have felt pretty awful if you hadn't went to the station. That's why I wanted you to go up home, so you could come along. That's the way it is, when you want the train to come late, it comes in right on the dot. The darned thing could have been four hours late and I'd have still made it with time to spare.

No, the Sergeants don't walk around with black books. I suppose its because they'd use up too many in a day with us fellows and they're doing their bit in saving paper.

I'll admit that at one time I did like Toad West, but that ended very abruptly when she started going with Dick Cochran. She went downhill very fast at that time.

But those days are gone forever. There's one girl I've liked a lot more than Toad for a longer time than said girl realizes. There were times I got very angry with this girl but I always got over it fast, maybe because I liked her too well to stay mad long. That girl is you, Anna. I don't believe I have any reason to be jealous now, but I'll admit I used to get green with envy of Hank. I'd see you two together and think "those two sure like each other, I guess there's no chance for me", and I'd feel pretty low. But now I think I have a chance and it makes me feel pretty good. I hope I'm not too optimistic.

I didn't have such a nice train ride because trains are getting very tiresome to me. The only one I enjoyed was the one taking me home and then I was mad because it seemed to be going so slow.

I went to the show last night, it was "Show Business" with George Murphy and Eddie Cantor. It was corny but not too bad. I didn't enjoy it to well. Maybe because something was missing. None of the fellows were even with me so I didn't have no one's hand to hold.

Well it's about time to close for lights out is five minutes. (Darn K.P.) . Anyway you're probably bored stiff now. So good night till tomorrow. Write soon and often. And don't forget I love you.

Dick

The comment about Hank is actually Grandpa's cousin Henry. So I guess those feelings really did linger for some sixty odd years, since that was how long it took for Grandpa to finally cut Henry out of the photograph with Grandma.

June 3, 1944
6:30 P.M.

Darling Anna:

Well I've been in Harlingen for almost another week now and its still the same old stuff. A bunch of boys from our barracks started school today so with luck I should start next Saturday.

I have bad news about that pin. I went over to the P.X. today and they don't have any of them. I'll keep after it though till they do get them and send it to you right away.

Today I was working at the B-B range. They have machine guns that shoot B-B's mounted in turrets. They have paper and wooden airplanes going around on a track and they shoot at them. I didn't get to try them out for they were too busy. I'd like to though for I'll bet it's a lot of fun.

I'd like to know what's wrong with my mail situation. Whether anyone's writing or if its just held up somewhere. I've only had two letters the whole week and those were from you. A guy gets pretty discouraged when he don't get mail.

I expect we'll have K.P. tomorrow but there's no list up yet so there's a good chance we won't. I believe that permanent detail is getting us out of it.

The Sergeant in charge of us is a pretty good egg. None of the work over there is hard, yet he takes five times as many guys as he needs. The morning I first got on he told the barracks chief he needed eight men. The chief said "there's fourteen for you". The Sarge said "good deal, give me twenty more". He got them. And on all those jobs you work about 20 minutes and loaf around the rest of the time.

Another time we were ready to leave on detail and the rest of the guys were getting ready for physical training. The Sarge said "you guys know you're supposed to have an hour's P.T. so I'll give it to you before we leave." He held up his middle finger and told us to do the same. Then he wiggled it up and down for a few seconds and said "that's enough, that's your P.T. for today." He's really a screwball.

I believe I'll go to the show again tonight. "Sailors Holiday" is on. You should enjoy that. Oh, that's right, you don't like the Navy as well anymore. I hope you're all for the Air Corps now cause there's a guy in there that goes for you in a big way.

Well, I'll close for now. Don't forget to write. I heard over the radio this afternoon that the invasion had started, then later that it was a false report. I sure wish it had been true for the sooner it starts the sooner this war will be over and we'll be together again. That's the day I'm looking forward to with all my heart. I miss you very much, Anna, and I love you very much too. So long for now.

All my Love
Dick

CHAPTER 5
D-Day Invasion and
the Continuation Gunnery School

On June 6th, 1944, the Allied invasion of Normandy had began with nearly 156,00 troops landing on the beaches in France. It was the largest amphibious invasion in history, attacking the Germans by land, air, and sea.

June 6, 1944
6:00 P.M.

Dearest Anna:
Today has been a wonderful day. First of all the invasion has started. I was woke up this morning by a fellow's radio blaring out the good news. You're right about wishing. I wished it would start soon and it did. I hope all my wishes come true as quick as that.

Second on this happy day I had no K.P. I went back on my power turret detail and just sat around all day.

Third and by far most important of all I got three letters from you today. I figured it had just been held up somewhere. I got one from Mom too. I believe everyone else has quit writing. I haven't heard from Gene since long before my furlough. I was just wondering today if maybe he isn't in on the invasion. Has he told anyone about his promotion yet? I don't give a darned if no one but Mom and you write, just so you write often.

43

You bet your boots I hate good-byes. There have been two good-byes especially I didn't enjoy and the last was the hardest. If we ever have to say good-bye again I'm afraid I won't be able to. When I get back I never want to leave you again.

You don't have to ask me if I want those pictures. You know darned well I do. Someday when I get a chance I'll have a good picture taken and send you. Or rather a picture, I'm afraid they would find it hard to do good with me.

Those days at home didn't merely fly. They went faster than a P-38. It's been almost two weeks since I left and those two sure seemed long compared to those at home.

You're not the only one who would need practice to go skating. Remember the time I skated with you and I would have to fall down. Well my skating hasn't improved any since then. If anything it's worse. I doubt very much if any girls would bother flirting with me, but if they would, I'd never notice them for I'd be too busy looking at you.

Are you sure you're not the jealous type? That's good for I'm afraid I do get slightly jealous once in a while. Several times I believe it was more than slightly when you were concerned.

I don't think I'd wear that overcoat home if it was 20 below. Did you ever hear of Sad Sack? Well that's what those overcoats make you look like. If I do get another furlough it's bound to be before winter for it will be after gunnery training. They have started giving them after training again but they may quit by the time I'm through if I get through. I want to make it now. I want wings, even if it's just gunner's wings. I doubt if it will ever be Sgt. Moore but it will probably be Corporal. Only with the invasion, the war may be over before that time, I hope.

That wish I made didn't come true yet, but it was a pretty big wish. It can't come true till I get home again, anyway. Since you're not supposed to tell the wish I guess I can't tell you, but your concerned in it.

You'll have to be careful on that bike. I like you much better in one piece. I was bumped off mine twice by cars so I should talk.

I've seen one girl in Phila. That has that girl beat, and I do mean you. And if you want your picture in Life just straddle the Tuscarawas River and have your picture taken. After all the Rio Grande is a much bigger river, if she could do it, you could.

I don't think it would be hard to find someone who wanted to marry you. You're the sort of girl a guy would be proud to have as a wife. And I'm not kidding.

You say you can't express yourself very well but I think you do a wonderful job of it. What good does a lot of words do? Just those words in shorthand mean the world to me as long as I know you really mean it.

You say you're love's not rationed. I hope you just mean that for me. I don't want to be selfish or anything but I want you all to myself.

You can rest your eyes for a while now for I'd better close. So till next time, so long. And keep those wonderful letters of yours coming. My morale is starting back to normal now. I love you.

Dick

It's interesting to read my Grandpa's reaction to the news of the Normandy Invasion. It shows how the long awaited invasion was perceived as a start to the end of the war, how they were unaware of the huge amount of casualties that were mounting up, and what a historical day it would become.

Pvt. Richard B. Moore
A.S.N. 35922674
Class 44-31
H.A.A.F.
Harlingen, Texas

Miss Anna Wyatt
208 St. Clair Ave. S.W.
New Philadelphia
Ohio

UNITED STATES
ARMY AIR FORCES

June 14, 1944
5:30 P.M.

Dearest Anna:

After getting two letters from you yesterday I didn't expect any today, but luck was with me and I did get one. So my morale is still up to 100%.

This morning we had lectures on first aid and malaria. I'll be a nurse too before you know it. But I'll bet some of the things they teach us are twice as gruesome as anything they taught you in nursing class.

This afternoon we shot the .22 rifle. I shot two whole boxes of shells. It was fun. They had little wooden airplanes running around on a track and you shoot at them. It's just like a shooting gallery. If you hit them they fall over. I didn't do too good but I'd hit one every once in a while.

After that we drilled for about an hour. We'd drill for about 5 minutes then take a 10 minute break so I didn't mind that so much.

46

To get to the lecture halls we have to march past the WAC area and there's usually a few WACs out there at noon in shorts or bathing suits taking a sunbath. The leader usually gives us "eyes right" and then we count WAC cadence. That's one-two and then whistle. You should here some of those wolves. (Of course, Moore is not included). I think they just sit out there to be whistled at.

They're getting rough down here now. Yesterday morning they weren't satisfied with the barracks at inspection so we had a stand-by inspection at 7 in the evening. Tonight they had a list of fellows who had something wrong at inspection today and they have to march tours tonight. Luckily I had everything all right so I don't walk but I'll be careful from now on so I won't have to.

Did you ever hear about some fellows getting letters about ten feet long or maybe longer? One of the fellows I run with got one tonight about four feet long written on both sides from his wife. I don't think I could write one that long. There's not that much to write about. I probably could keep telling you what I think of you and how much I love you, but I think just a regular letter would be enough.

Mary sure has tough luck. It seems like everything happens to her.* The joke was on you when you felt good because it wasn't your teeth. I think you should have it fixed though. A civilian dentist isn't so bad. He takes his time and does a good job and don't hurt you so much. But these Army dentists. They hurry and don't care if they drill clear through the roof of your mouth and they do a poor job all around.

It was exactly one month ago that I was pulling out of Columbus heading for Dennison. It seems like six months though. I hope with all my heart the next time I come home it will be for good for saying good-bye becomes harder to do each time.

It is funny the way memories come back. It rained a little today and it reminded me how every time we went out it rained and how mad we'd get.

But I don't need anything to remind me of you. I think of you all the time and of the swell time I had on my furlough while I was with you.

I don't know what made him say it, but the other day a fellow said "Moore, I think you're homesick for that girlfriend of yours." I don't know if you could call it homesick, but I am awfully lonesome for you.

I'll close for now. I may go to the show tonight and I have to clean up yet. So long for now and write soon. I love you –

Dick

*Mary is my Grandma's younger sister.

I remember Grandpa would tell me this story about inspections. One day they had a new Sergeant coming through who was a real hard ass by reputation. And one of the guys in his barracks had all these posters of pin-up girls all over the back corner by his bunk, which they weren't allowed to have up. So when the Sergeant walked into their barracks, he looked straight ahead, and walked directly to the back corner. He took a few good looks at all the photos of the ladies, turned around, and said "Looks good to me boys" and walked out. My Grandpa would smile and say, "Oh boy, did we think that was funny!", and he would slap his hand onto the kitchen table and laugh.

Dearest Anna:
I had an extra special surprise at mail call tonight. I got your letter with the pictures. Thanks a million. They're really swell. I've got my billfold full of your pictures now. And it improves its appearance very, very much.

This morning we had P.T. and drill. That drill was a laugh. We were to drill from 9 to 10. We left for the drill field about a quarter after 9. As soon as we got there the flight leader said "take a break", so we rested for about 15 minutes, then we drilled for five minutes, he said take a ten minute break and we'll go back to the barracks. So we got a full five minutes drill out of it. That's tough, isn't it?

This afternoon we signed the payroll. That took till 3:00. Then we were supposed to go out and shoot the .22 rifle some more but when we got out there they said it was too late, so we headed back for the barracks again. It's been a very rough day.

I saw a very good show last night. It was Jack Carson in "Make Your Own Bed." I haven't laughed so much since "Private Hargrove". Don't miss it.

I heard today that they bombed Japan again with the new B-29 super bomber. Boy, if they keep after those Japs with them they'll blow the whole island off the map.

I'm practically praying I get on a B-29. They told us that training on B-24s didn't mean we'd be on them in

49

combat and I'm darned glad of that for it's the last ship I want on.

I've never seen a B-29 on the ground but I've seen them fly over. I guess it's really a wonderful ship.

It's been so long since I've had strawberries that I forget what they taste like.

I saw "Jane Eyre" a long time ago. It was about the first week I was at Lubbock. It was a pretty good show only Orson Welles is a ham deluxe.

I doubt if I'll take two years to make Cpl. now, but I still hope the war's over before I do. I sincerely hope I'm not in the army two years. Just think the 18th will make six months. A lot of guys would still consider me as a rookie but it seems like an awful long time to me.

So you admit being jealous. I admit just trying to make you jealous. Such as the time Teresa G. was playing football when we were in Pauline's and I went out to play too. I said it was just because she was playing, but that wasn't so, for I never was interested in her. I doubted if you would care and maybe you didn't then but maybe you would now. (I hope).

I'll tell you one time I was very jealous. It was that night down at the depot when you had a sheet of paper and said your boyfriend's name was on it. Of course, I wasn't satisfied till I took it from you and seen who it was. My hopes went way down when I seen Henry Goudy on there. You were very mad at me that night too for looking at the paper.

I used to really get mad at you. I say to the devil with her, I won't even pay any more attention to her. But the next time I'd see you I'd forget about being mad and fall for you all over again. I must have it bad for I never could stay mad at you.

We ought to make a resolution never to get mad at one another again, but I'm afraid it wouldn't work. Just look how mad we got that night on the furlough when we started making those lists. The only good part about that was when we made up.

If I would give you a hint about that wish I might as well tell you the wish and I don't want to take any chances for it's one wish I want to come true more than I ever wanted anything in my life.

I always said I believed anything you told me and that's one thing I really want to believe. You have told me things that I hoped weren't true. When I say I love you, I mean it with all my heart, darling, for rest assured I'd never lie to you either.

All my Love
Dick

Grandpa was a tail gunner in a B-24 Liberator while he was fighting in the Pacific. He would always say how it was his favorite airplane. Though he laments about how much he doesn't like the B-24 in his letter, he did eventually fall in love with it. Perhaps he had more appreciation for it during all those hours in the air or maybe he just had really fond memories of it. But no matter what the reason was, he did love that airplane. I do find it surprising that after all those years of hearing him talk about the B-24 that he didn't want to be on one in the first place.

Grandpa was in the Army for two years. Perhaps he should have stopped writing his "I hope not" wishes down, because they are exactly what ended up coming true.

THE FOUR FLYING HORSEMEN'   U. S. ARMY AIR FORCES

PILOT, NAVIGATOR,
BOMBARDIER,
GUNNER

June 16, 1944
1:00 P.M.

June 16, 1944
1:00 P.M.

Dearest Anna:

Today is our last day of processing. This morning we seen some movies and had a couple lectures. This afternoon we look over our records to see that there's no mistakes on them. Tomorrow we'll move to the student area and then Monday we get down to business.

I'm writing now for we have to go to a chemical warfare lecture at seven tonight so I don't suppose I'll have time. Just think, we sat around from 7:30 to 9:30 waiting to see those training films. We could have had the lecture then and have tonight off, but no, that's not the Army way of doing things.

3:00 P.M.

Well, I'm back again. I've had my records looked over and everything is in order. That is all but one thing. I had my last tetanus shot at Lubbock, but they didn't mark it down so I had to take the shot again today. I made sure it was marked this time though. I'm safe from it for another six months.

Boy old Major Grumline sure fixed us up when we left Lubbock. He put on our service records – [Character-excellent. Efficiency as a soldier – excellent.] I guess he didn't know me any to well or he wouldn't have written that. He also put "highly recommended for the good

52

*conduct ribbon". That convinces me he don't know what
he's saying.*

*It also has that I'm a volunteer flight trainee "grounded
without prejudice for convenience of the government".
There may not be any prejudice on their part but there's
plenty on my end of the line.*

*Well, darling, this will have to be short. There's nothing
new except that I love you and that's been news for a good
while. At least to me.*

All my Love
Dick

*Pvt. Richard B. Moore
A.S.N. 35922674
Section N
Class 44-31 Brks. T-225
H.A.A.F.
Harlingen, Texas*

*Miss Anna Wyatt
208 St. Clair Ave. S.W.
New Philadelphia
Ohio*

*June 17, 1944
3:00 P.M.*

Dearest Anna:

Today's the big moving day. I've never moved as many times at all the other camps put together as I have at this one. The devil of it is we packed our barracks bags and set them out for the truck to pick up. They put them on the open truck and it started pouring down. All my clothes will be soaking wet now. It sure picks the darnedest time to rain.

This morning we had our orientation lecture on going into gunnery. The same old stuff. What a fine field this is and how we'll really like it before we leave. I've been here two months now and I wish those guys would go to Lubbock for a while and find out what a fine field is really like.

I've been assigned to the Martin turret. That's the top turret. It's about the best there is so I'm pretty lucky. Of course in combat the radioman will take that one so I'd probably get a waist gun there and that's the worst position on a ship. The top is the warmest turret on the ship. I doubt if it's the safest, in fact, none of them are what you'd call safe.

This afternoon we had our picture taken with a flying helmet, "Mae West" life preserver and parachute on. They send it to the hometown newspaper when you graduate so I may have my map in the "Daily Times" in a couple months.

The biggest event of the afternoon though was mail call. I had a letter from you and it was very encouraging.

We got one of our school books too. It's the main one about .50 calibers and turrets. Just like going back to high school again, only it will be a lot more interesting and much shorter in duration.

A week from tomorrow we get a ride in a B-24 to get the feel of it. That'll be my first plane ride. I hope Sunday rolls around pretty fast.

Thanks a million for the four-leaf clover. It come just in time too for I'll need lots of luck from here on. I think I'm

*plenty lucky anyway to have you for a girlfriend. I don't
believe there's a luckier guy in the states in that respect. I
couldn't hope for anyone better.*

*I hope we hear from Gene soon too. I wrote to him
again last night. I found his last letter and it was just two
months ago since I heard from him. That's a long time
without any mail from him.*

*I'm glad you made your mind up the way you did. It
makes me feel a lot better. And the way morale is around
this place I should needed bolstering up. I've never seen a
camp as gloomy as this place is anymore. I think it's the
mail situation too. The mail's been coming in pretty slow.
Mine's coming in all right for me, but the last couple mail
calls they've only had about twenty letters. And that's not
much for a whole barracks. No mail sure knocks a guy for
a loop faster than anything.*

*They told us we may get a delay en route furlough when
we graduate but not to count on it too much for they might
get orders to cut them out anytime.*

5:00 P.M.

*We were called out and moved while I was writing. My
stuff didn't get wet at all. The bags must have been pretty
well covered by others. Our new barracks are the same as
our old except they have tables for writing and studying.*

*I don't know what I'll do tonight. Maybe go into town
for a change, maybe go to the show. Sabre, the old
Harlingen gunner, is on in "Cobra Woman".*

*I guess I'd better close for now for I have to unpack and
get settled a little bit.*

So long for now, honey and write soon.

All my Love
Dick

P.S. New address again.

55

As I was reading this letter, I realized that the newspaper photo he was talking about was in a frame on the shelf behind me. And I thought, I know exactly which one he's talking about.

WILLIAM D. BRAINARD LOUIS T. CAMDEN RALPH A. BURKLEY ROBERT KING

TED D. KUEMMERLING WAYNE K. LAUGHLIN RICHARD B. MOORE RICHARD E. SHUFF

OHIOANS WIN WINGS. These Ohio aerial gunners have received their wings at the Harlingen (Tex.) Army Air Field. Two from Akron are Pfc. Ralph A. Burkley, son of Mr. and Mrs. C. J. Burkley of 1857 Goodyear Boulevard, and Pfc. Robert King, son of Mrs. Nettie King of 465 Hillwood Drive. Pfc. William D. Brainard is the son of Mr. and Mrs. Olive Brainard of Farmdale, Trumbull County. Pfc. Louis T. Camden's parents are Mr. and Mrs. Dallas N. Camden of Martins Ferry. Pfc. Ted D. Kuemmerling's home is in Canton, where his parents, Mr. and Mrs. Karl Kuemmerling live in the Avondale section. Mr. and Mrs. P. K. Laughlin of Salem are the parents of Pfc. Wayne K. Laughlin. The parents of Pfc. Richard B. Moore are Mr. and Mrs. Byron C. Moore of New Philadelphia. Pfc. Richard E. Shuff is the son of Mr. and Mrs. Charles B. Shuff of Tiffin.

ment of 7,000 striking General Motors employees pending negotiation of their dispute.

* * *

WILMINGTON, Del., Aug. 12— (AP)—A five-day walkout of 950 employees of the Worth Steel Co., Claymont, Del., is expected to end Monday, with mills resuming full operation, company officials said today. A plan for settling a wage

June 18, 1944
3:00 P.M.

My Dearest Anna:
I've been catching up on my writing today but it wouldn't be complete until I wrote to you.

It's Sunday and my day off and raining to beat the band so there's nothing else to do but write.

I saw "Cobra Woman" last night and it stunk. If it hasn't been there yet, don't waste your time seeing it.

Everything's so dead around here today, but then it's dead all the time I'm away from you. I'd give anything if I were with you today. We could go skating maybe, then to the show tonight. The day we can be together again will be a great day for me and I'm sure looking forward to it.

I suppose you'll be swimming today. We may be taught to swim here, during P.T. classes. I hope so, then we can go swimming. You know you picked a heck of a boyfriend. Can't swim, can't dance, can't drive, can't do much of anything in fact. But he does love you very much and misses you something awful.

I'm going to be kept pretty busy from now on, Anna, and maybe some days I won't get much chance to write, but rest assured, I'll try my best to write everyday.

That's another reason I'm trying to catch up on all my writing today. I think I've written close to a dozen now. From now on I'm not writing to anyone who don't write to me.

This is a very short letter, darling, but I just wanted to let you know I still miss you. So long and write soon.
All my Love
Dick

June 19, 1944
8:00 P.M.

Dearest Anna:

I'm so tired tonight I can hardly hold this pen. I think this is the hardest day I've ever put in since I've been in the Army. I hate to think what I'll feel like at the end of the week. If it wasn't for the plane ride next Sunday I think I'd sleep the whole day. I can see after just one day that this gunnery business will be no snap.

We got up at 5:30, ate chow, cleaned the barracks for inspection and fell out for classes at 7:15. We had classes from 7:30 to 12:30, had one hour for dinner and then classes from 1:30 to 4:30. We then had 10 minutes to change to P.T. clothes. There we had about 40 minutes calisthenics and run around the track once. Then we got back about a quarter to six had 10 minutes to take a shower and change to khakis to stand retreat. That was over at 6:30. By the time I had chow it was 7:30. So it has been a rather full day.

I don't think I would feel so tired except about the middle of the morning I started feeling dizzy and by noon I was sicker than a dog. So instead of eating I lay down till afternoon classes. That made me feel better and by 3:30 I was O.K. It's a good thing I felt better by P.T. time or I'd surely have passed out doing those exercises. I believe it was the heat for this is one of the hottest days we've had yet. I know it was that for at home I hardly ever sweat no matter how hot it got, yet today in those classrooms my shirt was wringing wet.

All these fellows who are in school now tell us how they lose weight, and I can readily see why that is.

We had classes on turrets, aircraft recognition, sighting, and tearing down the .50 calibre today. You have to learn the names of every little part on the gun, and the trouble is some of the smallest parts have the longest names. I can see where I'll have to do plenty of studying to get through. You know after we've learned to tear it apart pretty well, we have to tear it down and put it together blindfolded with gloves on. I was just wondering what the devil it's going to look like when I try it. Anything but a machine gun, I imagine. I'll probably have a dozen pieces left over.

There will sure be a lot crammed into these six weeks. More than I even realized before. So I'll have to keep on the ball to get it all I guess.

I wouldn't mind it at all if they weren't so darned unreasonable. Those officers stand around all the time just waiting for somebody to slip up in something. Such as talking in ranks or other little things like that. It seems like they have nothing else to do and they seem to take a delightful pleasure in pulling a guy out of ranks and chewing at him for ten minutes for not being at strict attention. For those cadets that's all right. I'd be willing to take all they threw at me if a commission was at stake but for a mere P.F.C. stripe. I don't know if I'll be able to stand it or not. I'm afraid if they ever start on me I'll tell them to stick gunnery and gladly be sent to the infantry.

I guess you're pretty tired of my griping by now. I'm sorry I picked on you but I had to unload to someone.

We'll get to the brighter spot now. I missed mail call and thought I was out of luck. But there is an R.L. Moore in the barracks and he got mine by mistake, so he looked me up and gave it to me. And the good part was I had two letters from you. That made me forget my tiredness. I guess no matter how low I get all I need is a letter from you to bring my spirits into high gear.

I also got a letter from Theresa G. I hope you don't mind my writing her. She made me promise to. All I consider her is a friend and her letter means nothing compared to yours. Besides your letters are much more interesting for the things you say sound wonderful to me.

I'll readily admit that I'm not any good at all for bike painting. Remember when I had all those pictures plastered over the fenders? And once I got started I didn't quit till I did an A-1 job of ruining too.

If I ever get those wings you can bet your boots you'll wear them. But don't count an awful lot on my getting them for after today I'm not too sure of ever wearing them myself.

I can imagine what your sunburn looks like for I've seen some beauts on the guys who go swimming here. That'll teach you not to stay out in the sun so long. I'd like to slap you on the back now and see how high you'd jump. As for laughing, I don't think I would for you'd look pretty wonderful to me sunburned or not.

I hope you enjoyed your trip to the dentist. (I can imagine that too.)

That guy wasn't kidding about Texas being a foreign country. This Sarge I used to work for in power turrets said he told some students he was drawing overseas pay for being in Texas and they believed him.

I don't know how soon after gunnery I'll go over. Some never do, others go over after a couple months transition in this country, and some have went to Hawaii right after training and took their transition flying there. I really wouldn't care if I went over if I got to see you again before I went.

I doubt if it will be over too soon but with all my heart I'm praying it is too, for the sooner I get back to you the better I'll like it.

You're not the only one who looks for the mailman. And as long as I keep getting such wonderful letters from the most wonderful girl in the whole world I think I can put up with this Army till the day I get to see her again.

61

I don't know if I will get to write as much anymore but I'll try my best even if they are short to let you know how much I still miss you. Even if I can't write you can still bet that I miss you terrible and love you very much.
All my Love
Dick

After reading the part about slapping Grandma on the back with her sunburn, it makes me wonder if all those times he did that to me, if it was actually on purpose. Because every time that I had a sunburn, you could bet on the fact that he would give my shoulder a loving squeeze or slap me on the back after a good laugh. Now I wonder if he was doing it to be funny and it wasn't by accident. I didn't jump that high, but it sure did hurt.

June 20, 1944
8:00 P.M.

Dearest Anna:
Well, another day is over and we followed the same schedule as yesterday. Only I don't feel as tired tonight for some reason. Maybe I'll gradually get used to it.
I can tear the gun down completely and put it together now but I'll need much more practice before I can do it blind folded.
Working on that power turret detail did help me for in turret class and sighting I could understand what the instructor was talking about much better.
I think I'll be able to stand 3 weeks of this. I don't suppose we'll be so rushed and the last week will be mostly flying and we won't be so rushed then.

A bunch of Chinese boys come in today. They held a bunch of our boys over from our class last Saturday to make room for them. They can't speak a word of English. They have to have an interpreter to explain everything in class. They're all Chinese Army Sergeants but they wear the U.S. uniform now. All of them look real young, about 16. I don't know if they're older or not. They must be pretty smart boys to be brought clear from China and be put through gunnery. I believe they're going to be cadets.

A fellow was saying he was outside the mess hall when they finished chow. Our Sergeant gave them "right face". The interpreter rattled off some Chinese lingo about a mile long and they did a right face. I haven't seen them marching yet but they say they're pretty snappy marchers.

I'm awfully glad you liked the bracelet. They still don't have the pins in and I saw those bracelets and figured you'd like that better. I don't see why Mom should give me heck, but I'm afraid if she wants one she's out of luck for that one of yours was the last they had. But maybe there's something there she'd like. I thought it looked a little big but wasn't sure.

Mom had no objections to my going with you anyway, and I most certainly see no reason why she should. Maybe you remember how she used to give me the devil every time she saw me talking to Toad. And I heard her say more than once what a nice looking girl Anna is. And I heartily agree with her on that point.

When we went to Dover to see my Aunt and Uncle, I was showing Uncle Art some of my pictures and he asked me who the girl was. Mom beat me to it and said "That's Anna, his girlfriend." He said "She's a very cute girl, Dick". So I guess everybody's agreed on that point.

I think you'll find, Anna, that Mom isn't as hard-boiled as she appears. She's a pretty good gal when she wants to be.

I certainly wish I were there to collect that kiss. Believe me when I get home I'm going to with interest.

I'm glad you finally got your bike painted. Now if you want to you can paint mine. Only I think that crate now needs more than paint. In fact all I need is a new bike.

I don't care if you write to Bradford. I know what it's like not to get mail, although the mail situation is coming along wonderfully now. I really don't know what right I'd have to stop you even if I wanted to. I don't blame him for wanting to hear from you, for I know what your letters mean to myself.

I guess we did slap one another around quite a bit. Maybe it could be classed as love taps. That sure is a funny way to show love though, isn't it?

I've been pretty lucky to get to write the last couple nights. I really should be studying now, but your much more important to me than a .50 calibre machine gun. I'll find time to study, but first I'll answer your letters. And I would feel very bad if you didn't write regularly. I don't know why I ever told you not to at Lubbock. I guess it was because you were so wonderful writing practically every day while I was neglecting my writing very much. I felt sort of ashamed of myself but I was glad you didn't take me serious for if you had stopped writing so often I would have missed those letters very much. So even if I can't write, you be sure to for your letters make mail call the happiest event of the day. And I like those long letters, don't ever worry about them hurting my eyes. They're the best eye medicine in the world.

I really must get some studying done tonight, darling. We have a test soon over the names of the parts of the guns and there's so many and the names are so long that they may give me trouble. If I flunk it would mean night school and I couldn't write at all. So I'll sign off and I can't help but have pleasant dreams for I always dream of you. Good night and I love you very much.

All my Love
Dick

Bradford may have been the other guy that Grandma was writing to. I remember her joking that she was writing to another fellow as well and Grandpa won out because he kept the letters coming. She also had a bag of coins from different countries in Europe that this same guy had sent to her while he was in the European Theater. Grandpa gave those coins to my Mom after Grandma's death because he didn't want them anymore.

The bracelet Grandpa sent to Grandma from Harligen, TX.

June 21, 1944
10:00 P.M.

Dearest Anna:
    It's rather late to start writing but I had a letter from you and decided to answer it tonight.

We have a test on the names of parts of the gun tomorrow so I studied for it first. I still don't know them very well but I'll just hope he asks us parts I do know.

To show you what I'm up against there's one little pin that can hardly be seen yet it bears the name "belt feed holding pawl locating pin". Awfully big for a little pin don't you think?

We had a test on aircraft recognition today. They flash them on the screen for one second. It don't sound like much time but they used to flash them at 1/100th of a second. I got 100% though. That's where all my fooling around with planes at home come in handy.

I tried tearing the gun apart blindfolded just for the fun of it today and I surprised myself at how easy it is. Aside from having to look once in a while to find a certain piece I did pretty well as far as actual assembly went. I don't believe that will give me as much trouble as I expected.

I finally run into someone I knew from Phila. It was Paul Edwards. I don't know if you knew him or not. He worked in Goshen Dairy. I went to school with him. We both tried for the Naval Aviation at the same time, he was rejected because he walked in his sleep.

He's a cadet yet. He's training to be a navigator. He graduates from gunnery Saturday. It's funny I didn't run into him before this.

I just wanted to surprise you with the bracelet. So I told you I had bought the pin.

If you think it's hot there, you should be here. I believe today's the first day of summer and it sure seems like it.

I got a letter from Joanne today and she didn't ask any questions. In fact she didn't say anything about you, which surprised me for she always asks me if I like you. Maybe she's sure I do now so she don't bother asking.*

I'm very tired tonight, Darling, so I'd better close and hit the sack. In P.T. today we run about a mile. It's a two

and a quarter course but we walked half of the way. So
good night for now, I just wanted to tell you that I love you
more than ever.

Love

Dick

* Joanne is Grandpa's other sister.

June 23, 1944
9:30 P.M

Dearest Anna:

Well only 36 more days to go before I'm a gunner.
These days are going pretty fast for we're so busy all the
time. I've been pretty lucky this week for I've been able to
write every night, but I'll probably be even busier next
week for they say the second weeks the hardest so maybe I
won't have as much chance to write.

Your letters have been coming in everyday too. I hope
they keep coming too.

We had a couple tests today and I passed both so I
won't have night school to take up my evenings. That's
O.K. with me too for we don't have enough time to
ourselves as it is.

Next week we'll have practically the same classes only
we'll have skeet shooting with the shotgun added in.

I'm getting a little better now at putting the gun
together blindfolded. I didn't have to look at all today.

I never did know the depot mailman's name. I wonder if
he's any relation to the Edwards boy I was telling you I met

the other day. So his wife likes you, well I can't blame her. It's not hard to do, for I liked you the first time I saw you.

I'll bet you don't even know the first time I saw you, but I do. It was in the Front Street school yard. You must have been in about sixth grade. Bob Alexander and I were walking home from high school. You were playing with some other kids and I remember asking Bob who you were. Little did I realize then how much I'd like you six years from then. In fact, I should say how much I'd love you.

So you like to be whistled at. Just so you don't encourage this whistling though. Just whose blood do you mean will be shed. I thought you weren't the jealous type (or are you). If I was walking down the street and wanted to whistle at some girl why should you mind?

Do you remember what else happened that night you were chasing me for that piece of paper. That was almost an embarrassing situation.

What's that saying about "true love never runs a smooth course"? Ours must be pretty true for it's had a pretty rough time. We never could seem to agree on anything.

I never used to study in study hall. I'd go over to the library or roam the halls. I don't know how I ever got through school with as little studying as I did. It just wouldn't work here for I do have to study now.

I used to hang around the library and my locker just to see you too. Sometimes I wish I were back in high school. I think I'd enjoy it more now.

I really must close now, sweetheart, for there's two tests coming up tomorrow. I must study, and I'm very sleepy. So it'll be a toss-up between sleep and study. I may just hit the sack for than I can dream of you longer. That's what makes sleep worth while.

All my Love
Dick

68

It was strange to read the well-known story about the first time Grandpa saw Grandma, since I had heard him tell me so many times. But in the letter he left out the funniest part where Bob calls her "Annie Whitecabbage".

UNITED STATES ARMY AIR FORCES

June 30, 1944
9:30 P.M.

Dearest Anna:

I'm rich again. Today was payday. I've got some cash to go to Mexico now. I wish you were here to go with me. We could have fun down there. I'll see it now while I got the chance for when this war's over I'm never coming around this part of the country again. If it can be called a part of our country. I hear they've been trying to give it back to Mexico but they figure the Japs and Germans are enough to handle now without bothering fighting the Mexicans.

I suppose you were burned up when you didn't have to wash clothes Monday. When I have work to do and something turns up to call it off it makes me pretty happy, but the trouble is it's still there to do the next day.

This week has really flew. It went even faster than the first week. I hope next week goes even faster. Next week at this time I'll be at the range or on the way there. I guess that's five times as bad as the camp here. There's no shade, there's twice as many varieties of bugs, plus a dozen other disadvantages. Guys gripe at the camp, but they're glad to see it after two weeks at the range.

That's quite a surprise about Miss Myer getting married. I guess you're never too old for marriage. Do you think you'll wait that long? I don't think so if I have anything to say about it. I can't see these secret engagements either. What's the use to get engaged if you don't tell anyone. If I was engaged to someone I really liked I'd be pretty proud of it.

It's a good thing your dad didn't go to work on the watch itself. That's the way I am with everything I try to fix. When I'm through it's fixed for good. I guess that's why I'm going to gunner school, for I'd make a mighty poor plane mechanic.

I guess there is a war on, that's what they tell me anyway. Only don't tell the draft board, it might give them ideas. (Or it looks like they already got the idea.) It's pretty hard to get what you want these days. I believe I did pretty good with the article entitled "girlfriend" though. I picked the best in that, although it was hard to convince her that I really cared for her. I hope she realizes that now.

I suppose this school is more important than high school and as far as this course saving my life some day, that's no understatement. That's why I'm working hard at it to get all I can out of it. As long as I'm going to be a gunner, I want to know what the score is. I want to keep those babies as far away from our bomber as possible.

I guess I'll close for now. I am writing as much as possible and I commend you on yours. I don't believe you missed a day this week and sometimes two a day. They're really welcome after a busy day in school. They'll be just as welcome out at the range if not more so, so keep 'em coming, darling. And I love you very, very much too.

Love
Dick

P.S. I saw this clipping in the paper, and thought you'd like to see it.

MINUTE TWO WAY Mail

By Russ Murphy

THE SOUTH BEND TRIBUNE, FRIDAY, JUNE 23, 1944.

The New Double-Duty Letter Game.
Boy checks ☐s and sends to girl.
Girl checks ○s and mails back to boy.
X marks the thought.

DEAR
[X]○ love-light
☐○ government man
☐○ friend
☐○ Joe

SINCE WE'RE APART I
[X]○ know it's love
☐○ get more sleep
☐○ ain't the same

(WHEW! X'D AGAIN)

☐○ do my own cooking

DID ANYONE EVER TELL YOU YOU'RE
☐○ handsome?
☐○ all mine?
[X]○ strictly a pin up?
☐○ tack-sharp and cream-smooth?
☐○ an all-right guy?

SATURDAY HERE IS
[X]○ no fun without you
☐○ really hot
☐○ just the day after Friday
☐○ pretty dull

THE FELLOWS HERE ARE
☐○ two jumps behind me
[X]○ O. D. (Outright Drab)

(WHOO-OO)

☐○ definitely drug-store
☐○ smoo-ooo-ooth!

PLEASE DON'T
☐○ wait
☐○ try to bribe the censor
[X]○ neglect to write
☐○ get hurt

THE GIRLS HERE ARE
☐○ two jumps ahead of me
[X]○ not as sweet as you
☐○ solid stuff
☐○ as lonesome as I

IN A FEW DAYS WE'LL BE
(SMACK)
☐○ together
☐○ older
[X]○ nearer the end

WHEN VICTORY COMES LET'S
☐○ take a long trip to the country
☐○ start sleeping late again
[X]○ make it stick

RHYME-A-LINE
Since we're apart,
It's love I miss,
But soon again
(It's you I'll kiss,)

P.S.

YOUR OWN
☐○ K. P. Kid
☐○ hug-bug
☐○ USO friend

MINUTE MAILERS ANSWER SAME DAY
Copyright 1944 by John F. Dille Co.

MARK UP — CUT IT OUT — MAIL IT TODAY

71

July 9, 1944
7:00 P. M.

Dearest Anna:
Another Sunday about gone, and another week starting tomorrow. Only three weeks to those wings. Cross your fingers, honey. You've brought me luck before, don't fail me now.
It's been a very boring Sunday. It's days like this I'd like to be back there with you, taking a walk, going to a show, skating. Anything as long as it was with you.
Now here I got up about 10:30, cleaned up and eat chow. Then there was nothing to do till two. Then I went to the show. After that still nothing to do. And I wanted to get in the Army to have something to do. There I am griping again. I gripe when I have something to do and gripe with nothing to do. I guess that's the way you get in the Army.
Remember how you used to say I'd probably change in the Army and never pay any attention to you when I come home? Do you think I changed? I noticed a few small changes in you. You were better looking than ever, and you'd pay some attention to me.
Our barracks is at one end of the field and when those planes take off they buzz right over. I'm glad they don't fly at night. I'd never get any sleep. The more I see of this place the more it reminds me of Keesler. Those old tarpaper huts. The same kind of mess hall, lines a mile long everywhere you go. Maybe I wouldn't want the instructor's job if it was offered. I think I'd be better off in a combat crew.
The show today was fair. Fred McMurray and Barbara Stanwyck played in it. The name was "Double Indemnity".

Stanwyck is a blond and she looks like the devil with light hair. It's a funny show. The two main players are both murderers, but it's still pretty good.

Some guys were around here talking about what they were going to do after the war. Some are going to get married and settle down, some aren't even going home again. I don't know what I'll do. Have you any ideas? Maybe I'd better wait till it's over. That settling down sounds pretty good though. Yep, it sounds darned good.

Well, tomorrow we'll probably shoot the .50 calibre. I hope I can hit something with it. I ought to hit more than two out of 250 anyway. Remember that cartoon I sent you of the guy shooting the gun? I suppose that's the way I'll be.

I guess I'll close for now. I'll write tomorrow and let you know how I make with it. I love you.

All my Love
Dick

July 17, 1944
7:30 P.M.

Dearest Anna:
Another day over and we still haven't went up. We're supposed to fly tomorrow for sure but I suppose they'll fool around and we won't go up again.

We fired from the Martin Turret mounted on trucks today. It's a lot more fun and I can hit more than with the hand held .50.

I shot 600 rounds, 200 at a time. Those 200 sure go through fast too. I don't mean that you hold the trigger till all 200 go through. You fire in bursts of about 12. You should see the barrel of a gun after someone shoots about 100 at a crack without letting up on the trigger. It has more curves in it than Mae West. I think if I can keep up on my score in the turret I can bring my average up to passing. Maybe that's just wishful thinking but I have my fingers crossed on it anyway.

If you want Babe or Clarence to go on the merry-go-round with you, just go ahead. It won't make me mad. I'm not the jealous type, you know. How the devil did Clarence ever get in there? I'd forgotten all about him, and believe me I was better off to forget him. We'd better be careful or we'll be fighting again like that night at home. I still can't figure out why we even started that. At least we had enough sense to not stay mad.

I wish we'd have some more rain out here. At least it gets us out of P.T. but this week they're going easy on us. They usually just give us a couple exercises and send us over the obstacle course.

I guess Joanne's not the only one who don't want us to get mad. Why should we, anyway. I wonder why she's so interested? I can't blame her for approving though. I think I've got a pretty swell girlfriend. How about you?

For what reason should I forget you just because I was in the Army? That's all the more reason to remember you. I don't think I could forget you if I tried. In fact, I know I couldn't.

You bet your boots I have some one special in mind to settle down with. Someone extra special. All I hope is that she's as willing to settle down as I am. You ain't kidding

I'm going to travel when the war is over. I'm going to travel straight to Phila. If I would have become a pilot and had a commission I might consider staying in, but now, I'm just waiting for the day I can get out. I don't think Gene likes it well enough to stay in, either.

I haven't heard from Theresa for over three weeks, and it don't worry me, in fact I never thought of it till you mentioned her. She's not a stranger in the same sense as Bradford. You haven't even seen him.

I guess that's all for now, honey, keep writing. I got two letters from you tonight so I'm in a pretty happy mood. So good night.

All my Love
Dick

Grandpa graduated from Gunnery Training on July 29th, a few days after the American troops completed the liberation of Guam, which had been captured and occupied by the Japanese for three years.

He left Harlingen on August 2nd for New Philadelphia for his delay-en-route, which granted him time off between his transfer from Texas to Nebraska.

CHAPTER 6
Casper Army Air Field, Wyoming
Combat Crew Training

On August 17th, Grandpa reported to Lincoln Army Air Field in Lincoln, Nebraska for assignment to combat crew. He left on September 10th for Casper, Wyoming, where he reported for combat crew training for practicing bombing and gunnery.

Pvt. Richard B. Moore
A.S.N. 35922674
Combat Crew Detachment
Crew #8362
Army Air Field
Casper, Wyoming

Miss Anna Wyatt
208 St. Clair Ave. S.W.
New Philadelphia
Ohio

ARMY AIR FORCES

Sept. 11, 1944
6:30 P.M.

My Dearest Anna:

Well, I'm here. It's dear old Casper. For once, the rumors were right. And oh how I wish they had been wrong. As soon as the camp come in sight I knew I wouldn't like the place. After I've been here four hours I know I won't like it. I'd like to have the guy here that told me Casper was such a swell place, I'd shove the words right down his throat.

The first thing they did was take us to the theater for talks introducing us to the field. And what talks. They smelled strongly of chicken shit (excuse the language please) from beginning to end.

Back at Lincoln you heard such wonderful things about O.T.U. Passes anytime you're off duty, no C.S., plenty of time off, live like kings. And most of the bases are like that. But no, we get a field like this. Gripe, gripe, gripe. If you get tired of my griping let me know. I'll let up on it now.

We'll start flying Thursday. We have to fly at least 6 1/2 hours a day, three days out of the week, the rest of the time is ground school on sighting, the .50 calibre, turrets, just further training on things we got at Harlingen.

So we won't have a lot of time off. We get one day off every 9 days and can get a pass for town the whole day. We just passed through Casper, but it looks like a pretty nice town. I think I'll go in when I get a chance. I supposed I've only got a couple more months in this country. I may as well get away from camp once in a while just for a diversion.

We'll be here for 2 1/2 months, then it's overseas, I don't know about furloughs out of here. I don't think we get them though. Of course, things could change before we get out of here.

I found out about our pilot. We'll get them here before we start flying, so everything will be all right there.

I met the rest of my crew. There's Noonan from Connecticut. He's the tallest, about 5'10". All the rest are shorties like me, I think I'm second tallest. Then there's Steppe, he's from South Carolina, a damned rebel. There's Angelino from New Hampshire. The last of the gunners is Spencer. He's the shorty, about as tall as Vince. I believe he's the Sperry Ball man, he's built for it anyway. I don't know where he's from. They seem like a pretty good bunch of fellows.

The chow is pretty good, they have permanent K.P.s here so that's one thing I don't have to worry about.

Lincoln was surrounded by hills. This place has a range of mountains on the one side. They look beautiful, just as long as our pilot keeps away from them and don't plow them up with our B-24.

They issued us two blankets so I guess it gets sort of chilly here. You're allowed to wear either summer or winter uniform. I'll have to get all my winter uniform dry cleaned and have it ready. Then I'll get my khakis cleaned and put them away for the winter. I'll have some cleaning bill this month. I'll probably have to send home for money.

We go through processing again. That's checking our clothes, physical exam, and checking our records again. The same old stuff we went through at Lincoln.

They've got one theater here and all the shows for about a week ahead are those I saw at Lincoln so I won't be going to a show for a while. Abbot and Costello's on tonight.

One encouraging thing they told us was that gunnery isn't as bad as it used to be. It used to be you could only expect about 50% of the crews to come back alive but now you can expect about 95% to make it alive. Also that this thing might be over before we have to go across. I hope he was right but you can't tell.

Well, darling, I suppose I'd better take a shower and clean up after that dirty train trip. I'll write more tomorrow and maybe I'll have a different opinion of the joint.

79

Remember I love you, more than I can begin to tell. The longer I'm in this Army, the more I want the day to come when we'll be together again. Good night, honey and pleasant dreams, don't dream like you did anymore. I wouldn't want anything like that to happen either.

Love forever,
Dick

    P.S. This gum is still from Lincoln. I don't know how the gum situation is here.

Pvt. Richard B. Moore
A.S.N. 35922674
Combat Crew Detachment
Crew #8362
C.A.A.F.
Casper, Wyoming

Miss Anna Wyatt
208 St. Clair Ave. S.W.
New Philadelphia
Ohio

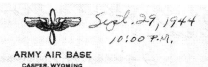

ARMY AIR BASE
CASPER, WYOMING

Sept. 29, 1944
10:00 P.M.

My Dearest Anna:
    Well, honey, we didn't fly today and I'm sort of glad for we've been flying too much to suit me this week. I don't mind about four times a week and we've already been up three times this week and a couple more days to go.

80

Instead we went out to the range and got a little ground firing. Then this afternoon we seen our films we took yesterday. Mine really turned out good. A lot better than I expected. I shot them from the waist too. I guess that old waist position is just made for me. Our bombardier was the only other one who fired. He got some mighty poor pictures. You can tell he's been out of gunnery school for a long time.

I hear the navigators come in today so we'll probably have ours next time we go up. That will complete the crew.

I guess the reason I never heard from you in five days was because the mail was balled up some way. One or two of them must have got lost somewhere. I hope it never happened again. I was ready to shoot up somebody. No kidding, I was getting desperate.

You think a fire feels good after school you should come in to a good old fire in the barracks after a high altitude mission. Then's when a fire really feels good.

I don't know how good I'd be at raising chickens, honey, but as long as it would be with you, I'd sure try awful hard. The chicken farm or the little cottage both sound good as long as it's with you. I'd like a little place like Millie and Flick has. Only no red porches, please. A red roof all right, but a more sensible color for the porch. They really have a nice setup there. You could even raise chickens out there. It sounds pretty good to me, darling, as long as I had you, I'd be perfectly happy any place. Chicken raising shouldn't be too hard, I think I could learn. Can you cook chicken? We'd have a chicken dinner once in a while with all those chickens. I can fry, boil and scramble eggs, so I could help out there. All we'd want would be chickens though and probably a dog. I'd want a job somewhere and it would be too much have a lot of other livestock.

81

Of course we couldn't leave the chicken out. We could have all three, cottage, chickens and children. How does that sound to you? It would take time though. I'd have to work a while to save enough money to get started.

Maybe I could save enough in the Army, but I doubt that. There's my war bonds too but then years is far too long to wait.

How does my idea sound? Does it suit you or have you a better suggestion?

We start flying afternoons again Sunday so there's no more of this getting up at three o'clock for another week. We go to ground school tomorrow and it's also payday. Do you want to go out and have a good time tomorrow night or should I put that big P.F.C. pay toward that cottage.

I guess that's all for now, darling, except to say again that I love you oh so much. I've said it again and again, but I mean it more every time. Good night, sweet, pleasant dreams.

> *Love Always,*
> *Dick*

Pvt. Richard B. Moore
A.S.N. 35922674
211th C.C.D. Crew #8362
C.A.A.F.
Casper, Wyoming

> *Miss Anna Wyatt*
> *208 St. Clair Ave. S.W.*
> *New Philadelphia*
> *Ohio*

Oct. 5, 1944
12:00 A.M.

My Dearest Anna:
I didn't get a chance to write yesterday honey. We flew till about eleven again last night.

We went to the air to ground range in the afternoon and fired there a couple hours. Then our radio operator got a bad case of air sickness and we had to come in to let him off. As we circled the field one of the fellows looked out and there about a mile from the runway was a plane burning. You could see where it had plowed across the highway and a few hundred yards past that.

The fire trucks were on their way out when we first saw it so it must have just happened. They had the fire out a couple minutes after they got there.

We landed and let our radioman off and then took off to drop some bombs. The bomb rack wouldn't work then and we couldn't drop any so we come back down.

We found out then it was crew 8360 that crashed. They are all in our barracks. Three of them were lucky they didn't go up. Then there were three not so lucky. As far as we can find out that's how many were killed. The rest are in the hospital. One of the fellows killed was a Tech Sergeant who had been a gunner in the South Pacific. He finished his missions there come home and signed up for a crew again. Then he gets killed in training. If I ever get into combat and come out of it, my feet are staying on the ground for the duration.

There was one fellow on the crew I got to know pretty well here. He was a swell fellow and from what they say he was just badly shaken up and will be O.K. I hope that's right too.

You know, I've come to the conclusion that if we get through this training O.K., we've got a pretty good chance coming out of combat alive.

So you're a bowler now. 95 is O.K. for a beginner. I believe I had 98 the first time I bowled. It's a deal, the next time I'm home we'll go bowling. They just opened up the bowling alley here. I'll get a little practice and show you how to bowl. It's been over two years since I bowled. It was before Gene went to the Army. It is a lot of fun, but I'm not much good at it.

So the trees are pretty now. I wouldn't know. I haven't seen a tree since I got here. This is the most desolate country I've ever seen. All we fly over is waste land.

It's too bad about that Doris. Infantile paralysis isn't a pleasant thing to have. Where did you ever get the idea that Anna Wagner is an old flame of mine? I never did like her. It was Hank that used to tease about liking her and I don't know why anyone thinks I did. I didn't see her when I was home either. In fact, I haven't seen her for a long, long time. I even forget what she looks like.

I guess I'll close for now, darling. We have to fly this afternoon and I have to get ready. Don't worry about me cutting myself shaving. I finally learned how to use one of those razors. So long, sweetheart. I love you, I love you so much. I'll be thinking of you while we're up this afternoon. But then, I think of you always.

Love Forever

Dick

A picture I found in Grandpa's photographs. I don't know if this is the plane he described or another one from somewhere along his journey.

Oct. 6, 1944
6:30 P.M.

My Dearest Anna:
You said you didn't mind my griping, well tonight I'm in the mood for it. It started yesterday. We went for briefing at 1:30. They didn't have enough planes so they told us we'd have to wait for one. Well, we had to sit around till 8:30. They come in and called for our crew. Everyone else was coming down already and we thought they were going to tell us to go. But no, they merely wanted to say they had a plane for us. Nice of them, wasn't it. By the time we were ready to take off it was ten o'clock. We only were up an hour, but I don't see why we had to go up at all.
The plane we had was the "Flying Shamrock". I believe it was the first B-24 ever built. It had been through combat until it was no good over there and then sent here for us to train in. If you ask me it should be the "Grounded Shamrock".

*There's some captain down here and he's C.S. deluxe.
But he gave us a good laugh last night. When we landed we
were turning in our parachute, he come running in yelling,
"is crew 8362 in here? The ones who were in operations
all afternoon?" We said yes, sir. He said "Did you see
anyone take a B-29 out of there this afternoon?" We looked
at him like he was crazy. "What was that sir? He said "Did
you see anyone take the B-29?" By that time we figured he
was off his nut. Then he said a model B-29. That sounded
sensible. He acted as though it was a calamity though.*

*Then today for further griping they had the schedule
mixed up. We were scheduled to go to the range this
morning so we went out there for a couple hours. Then they
come and told us we weren't supposed to be out there till
this afternoon, so we had to go out again this afternoon.
Then it turns out today is supposed to be our day off. The
first one in two weeks.*

*Sometimes I get pretty disgusted with this army. In fact
I've been pretty disgusted with it for quite a while.*

*You know, today I got a letter from you dated Sept. 16.
That's another gripe. Not getting the letter for it's far from
a gripe to hear from you, but I'm griping because it took so
long getting here. No wonder I didn't hear from you for five
days.*

*Honey, I don't ever intend getting interested in that girl
from Dennison. More than likely she would be a
disappointment, but even if she looked like Hedy Lamarr
she wouldn't interest me. There's only one girl I'm
interested in or ever will be. I've said it many times and
will say it many more. That girl is you, sweetheart and I
mean it. Who would care about some girl in Dennison
when they had a top-notch girl like you? I may be pretty
dumb about lots of things, but I'm smart enough to realize
what a swell girl you are.*

There's no need smuggling me any bars. I don't care a whole lot for candy anymore and they have a few at the P.X. Gum is impossible to get here too. At Lincoln they always had plenty but here they haven't had anything but that cheap stuff for a couple weeks.

The cake was in fairly good condition. The one side of it was a little smashed but outside of that it was O.K.

Finishing ahead of schedule won't mean shipping out any sooner. It may mean a furlough though and that's what I'm hoping for. If we do finish before time and don't get home, we'll probably lay around here till Nov. 30 before leaving for a staging area. I'm hoping for the furlough though, honey, so it's better to finish ahead of time.

Yesterday during briefing before flying the Lt. Got up and said "Lt. Burns, please stand." That's our pilot. Then he told all of us gunners to leave and the officers to stay. It seems they wanted to make an example of Burns. He beat up a couple M.P.s the night before. They fined him $75 for it. Burns is a pretty good Joe. In the air, he's dead serious, but on the ground he's a regular guy. He jokes and cuts up along with the rest of us. That's the kind of pilot to have.

We've lost our radio operator now. He's being grounded because he gets sick in the air all the time. He's been up 32 times and sick 32 times. I'm afraid if I'd get sick every time I went up I'd stay on the ground too. I've been O.K. the last 4 or 5 flights, so I don't think it will give me any trouble.

I guess I've run down for tonight sweetheart. I believe we have ground school tomorrow so I'll be able to write tomorrow night. Good night, my darling, and as always, I love you, very, very much.

Love forever,
Dick

P.S. That old letter I got today was the one in which you had little hope for our team this year. Aren't you ashamed of yourself, after seeing what the "runts" can do? Good night again sweet. I love you.

My Grandpa used to tell me the story of when he would get airsick during training. He used to get it pretty bad when he first started, so he went to the doctor and told him that he was getting air sick. The Army said that maybe Grandpa wasn't cut out to be in the Air Corps. After that conversation, he never got air sick again.

Oct. 20, 1944
2:30 P.M.

My Dearest Anna:

It sure is a beautiful day out. The sun's shining bright, it's nice and warm. It's more like a spring day than autumn. We have nothing scheduled to do today so I've been loafing around. Right now I'm laying on the sack answering the wonderful letter I got from you today. You see it's a perfect day all around.

Now I can write a few letters, go to evening mail call, eat supper and go to the show. We don't do anything till 12:30 tomorrow when we fly, so I can sleep in tomorrow morning. You see what a nice life we lead in the Army, not a care in the world. Only days like this don't come around very often.

What do I mean not a care in the world? I have one big care and that's the fact I'm so far away from you. Oh well, this war can't last forever (I hope).

So you're bowling is improving now. What do you mean not much? So it's only five points but it is an improvement. Before you know it you'll be bowling in the 200s, maybe.

I don't believe I did see "Follow the Boys". If it's as bad as you say I'm glad I missed it. There's a hillbilly show on tonight. I'll probably go for want of something to do, but I've got a feeling it's going to be plenty corny.

You bet your boots I wouldn't like it if Babe would kiss you goodnight now. I didn't know he was actually your boyfriend then. You didn't have your way pretty much of the time, you had it all the time.

I remember how the gang used to go for hikes to Indian Hill about this time of the year. Sunday afternoon with nothing to do, we'd have a lot of fun hiking. Of course that was a couple years ago. Last year this time Hank, Vince, and myself were about the only ones to go. The rest were either in the Army or working somewhere. We used to raid Graff's orchard all the time. Today seems like Sunday to me. It would be perfect for a hike. Only there's a much bigger hill to climb out here, and no apple trees to raid.

If we didn't go for a hike we'd always have a football game going. I really made you mad the time I tackled you in Pauline's yard. You were a perfect target standing there though, and I couldn't resist it. You didn't know what hit you. Then when you did find out, you were ready to murder me.

I'll close for now, darling. I'm going over now and see if I'm lucky enough to have another letter from you today. So long, sweetheart, I love you. I love you more than anything else in this world, and I miss you terribly much. I can't wait for V-day, either, my darling, it will be one of the happiest days of my life. The happiest day will be after victory when I come back to New Phila. to you forever.

Love Always
Dick

Nov. 11, 1944
11:00 P.M.

My Dearest Anna:

As you see I got some more wild west stationery. I wrote Vince a letter on toilet paper today and told him that's how bad the stationery was here. I just did it as a joke.

I'm lost as to what's going to happen to our crew now. We're right back where we were at the start, without a pilot. I don't know what's wrong with that guy. You remember I told you he beat up a couple M.P.s and was court-martialed and fined $75? Well, last week he was *absent from briefing and the co-pilot covered up for him and said he was sick. Well, they check up and he was sick all right. He was lying in his sack drunk. So he's up for court-martial again, he's been taken off the crew and put in the pool and I don't suppose he'll be put back on. It's going to cost him 3 or 4 hundred dollars this time and I wouldn't be surprised if he lost his commission.*

I sure hate to lose him as a pilot, the whole crew hates it too. Despite his liking for liquor he's a wonderful pilot. He's so cool and calm flying that thing, even in close formation where you have to keep on your toes all the time. You couldn't ask for a better pilot, he's the kind of guy you could go into combat with and feel you had a good chance coming back. If I ever start drinking I hope someone shoots me, drink's ruined many a man.

I don't know what will happen to the rest of us. They may split us up and put us on different crews and that would burn me up good. So far we haven't been put in the pool yet.

Again they may just give us another pilot. If they do that we'd probably have to go through this whole training again. That would make me very happy. I can see myself sweating out these beat up 24's these winter months at Casper. I wish I knew just what we'll do. To top things our co-pilot is in the hospital, for what I don't know. He had to have x-rays taken, if they find something physically wrong with him he'll be grounded for good.

So you're going to be a working girl now. I'll drop in Newberry's and buy something off you someday. I'll bet you make a good sales girl. You should increase their business 200% at least.

If I was home with you all to ourselves on that nice couch, I wouldn't complain about there being no fire place. I'd be pretty happy just being with you.

Your day dreaming sounds awful good to me and not crazy as you say. It makes me wish I was there and we were making plans to go out with Gene and Ethel. That would be perfect, darling, if we were all home and could go out and have a good time. I wish this were celebrating this war's armistice today instead of no. 1. Then maybe all our day dreams wouldn't be just dreams but actual facts. We'll have a lot of fun together when this war's over, honey, I promise. All our dreams will come true, the chicken farm, Karen Ann, Dick Jr. and all the others.

I sent you those wings because I wanted you to have them and because I promised, but mostly because I wanted you to have them. Now don't go telling me you won't take them. You're supposed to give them to the person you love and heaven only knows how much I love you. I want you to have them darling and only you. If I hadn't been so damned absent-minded all this trouble would have been avoided by giving them to you before I left.

I guess I won't be seeing you as soon as I hoped. Maybe I won't be going over as soon as I expected either. I know I won't be able to give you the wings in person, because they're already in the mail and you should have them by now.

It's getting pretty late, darling, so I'd better close. We don't have anything scheduled for tomorrow so I'll be able to write again then. Good night sweetheart, I love you, I'll always love you.

> *Love forever,*
> *Dick*

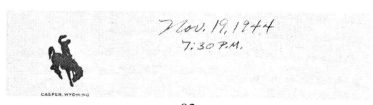

Nov. 19, 1944
7:30 P.M.

CASPER, WYOMING

Nov. 19, 1944
7:30 P.M.

My Dearest Anna:

I'm terribly sorry for not writing the last couple days but I just didn't have time. As I had expected, with a new pilot we'd be flying every time. We have flown the last three mornings and have been up 7 and 7 1/2 hours every time. With so little sleep and so much flying I'm ready to hit the sack and sleep for a week. We wouldn't have flown yesterday but our new boy, Capone is eager or something for he practically begged for a ship and so they give us one and we flew.

Friday we finished all our bombing and had a little formation. You can tell Capone has had quite a bit of time in Libs for he's as good as Burns. You should have seen them today. I think they were trying to see who could fly the tightest formation. We practically had our wing tip in the waist window of the ship beside us. I could go into combat with those two and know that if I didn't come back it wouldn't be their fault. But I'm afraid when we go overseas they won't waste a good pilot like Burns as a co-pilot. They'll probably make him first pilot with another crew.

The first day we flew Burns was sort of sulky and down in the mouth about having been made co-pilot, but the last couple days he's been in the best humor I've seen him in since we hit Casper. Maybe he was just worrying before whether or not Capone was any good.

Yesterday we went on our 1,000 mile cross-country to Great Falls, Montana. All there was to see was snow, so I slept practically the whole flight. I believe we'll have one more cross-country.

The pursuit ships come in again so today's mission was camera gunnery. I had a field day today. I got into the turret, put the magazine of film in and fired away, I had

93

that run through in ten minutes. I pulled it out and our engineer shoved another magazine to me. This went on till I fired 5 magazines. I was only supposed to fire two. I fired both the engineers and one of the radioman's. I'd get the sights on the pursuit ship and hold the trigger down till it was out of range, fire about half the film in one burst. The gunnery instructor called on the interphone and asked how many feet of film left? He thought I was still on the first one. I told him I'd just put my third magazine in and he was sort of surprised. I hate to think what those pictures look like. I got about a dozen B-24's I'll bet, and that's not good. That was silly for if they're too bad I'll just have to do it over again.

We start our processing tomorrow. Another clothing check, physical exam and record check. Will be leaving about the 29th or 30th and that's just getting ready. We won't get any furlough from here, that's sure now.

I thought I told you I was kidding about that long engagement stuff. My god, if I waited that long I might as well not get married.

You know darned well I was only kidding when I used to "insult" you. I just liked to see you burn up.

It don't look as though I will be able to see the Dover game with you. Maybe next year we'll be able to see all the football games. I hope so anyway. It's almost a year since I've been in the army and another year is far too long to be in. I don't blame Tommy for asking for 10 extra days if he could get it. If I were in his shoes I wouldn't stop with asking for only 10 days.

You're not kidding it's hard to get cigarettes. All they have here now is Ralieghs and they aren't any good. They only get good ones about once a week and they're gone in a few hours. I don't know what's causing such a shortage. A guy here with a pack of Camels is a very popular guy.

I know a Peggy Spittle but I never knew anything about her liking me. I worked with her Dad down at the Ladel, but I never knew her very well.

That's rough when you don't get a full nights sleep, believe me I know. The last three nights I've been lucky to have nine hours sleep. Boy, it's going to be wonderful to sleep till 8 in the morning.

I forgot to tell you, but we've got a daring young man on the flying trapeze on our crew. Noonan, the Sperry ball man was in his lower turret firing at the pursuits. He was leaning against the door of the turret when all of a sudden it felt as though there wasn't any door there. He looked around and by golly, there wasn't any door. It had come open and the slipstream had taken it right off. So there he was nothing between him and 20,000 ft of space but a little safety belt. He pushed forward on the controls and brought it up in the ship and got out of it fast. If that would ever happen to me I'd still be cleaning my pants.

Well, my darling, I guess I've bored you long enough with all these details about flying but it's something to fill up space till I say that I love you. After all that's the most important thing to me – my love for you. Everyday brings us closer to the day we'll be together again, but oh, how long the days are. Good night, sweetheart, I love you.

Love always,
Dick

Not only did Grandpa pass on his love of airplanes to me, but he also passed on his love of cinema and photography. Grandpa was always into photography, buying every kind of camera. He had quite a collection of cameras starting in the 1940's through the 2000's.

When he said he had a field day filming the pursuit planes, I bet he wasn't kidding. He loved those airplanes and getting to film them in flight probably made him so happy. I wonder if his love of photography started in the back of that B-24.

When I was eight, he had purchased a VHS camcorder that he would let me use. I can't believe he trusted me with it since I was so little, but I loved using it. That is probably what motivated me to want a career in film and television. And to think, now I'm the one who is filming out of B-24s and other WWII aircraft.

I have shot out of a B-24 and a B-25 bomber for a television series, so I could relate to how Grandpa felt filming out of a WWII bomber and worrying if the pictures would actually turn out. Those planes can toss you around with all the bumps. It's hard to focus and get a steady shot for more than a couple of seconds. I do wish I could have shared those stories with him. He would have gotten such a kick out of it, since he had once had the same experience. I can just see him saying "oh boy", slapping his hand on the table, and remarking that "your Grandpa did that too". He would have been so happy.

Nov. 20, 1944
10:00 P.M.

My Dearest Anna:
I was very lucky today. I had two letters from you, so I have no complaints at all. I told you about the mail system.
I thought we'd have to go through this training again with a new pilot, but it don't look that way. You see all the crew members have to have a certain amount of training. A

pilot has to have so many hours of formation flying and a good bit of instrument practice even if he's been flying for 10 years. I still don't understand why our new pilot don't have to get this training, I'll admit he don't need it, but still he's supposed to have it. In combat if you got a new pilot he would have had that training so he could be put right on the crew and ready to go into combat.

We can have pictures of the crew taken this week. The pilot has to make arrangements. Capone's new here, so he probably don't know about it. We'll have to hunt him up tomorrow and get him over there. Spencer, our nose gunner, knows a WAC over in the Photo Lab pretty well so he may be able to talk her into making some extra prints of the picture.

So you're the kind of girl that gives teachers trouble are you? Aren't you ashamed of yourself? I'd like to give Caroll some trouble myself. He thinks he still runs the school. They should have kicked him clear out of Phila. while they were at it. I never really hated a teacher as much as him.

I liked Miss Beaber, though. She always used to give me the devil for running out of the room when the bell rang. I always did that to get up the stairs before the crowd come down. She hardly ever loses her temper. I don't know how she had so much patience with our English class.

You sure have lots of trouble with that coffee pot. We'll have to have a metal one. You don't think they'd blow up do you?

I saw where Phila. rated among the first ten in Ohio, but I thought they were sixth. Seeing the record of the others I think they should be second or third at least. I hope they take care of Canton all right.

I don't have anything to do tomorrow so I think I'll catch up on some of that sleep I've been missing this week. I'm pretty sleepy now so I'd better get a good start.

We processed today, we'll be leaving in about ten days. I wish I knew if I were getting home before going over so I could put my mind at ease. I want so much to see you again first for I love you very much, Anna, very, very much. Good night, honey and pleasant dreams.

Love forever
Dick

ARMY AIR BASE
CASPER, WYOMING

Nov. 24, 1944
11:00 P.M.

My Darling Anna: <u>I love you</u>

   I didn't get to write last night, because we flew yesterday. We had camera gunnery again. There are only two more flying days for us. Sunday and Tuesday and probably we'll only fly one of them. Our stay at Casper is growing shorter and shorter.

   It started snowing again this afternoon. Not very much but it will probably snow more tonight. My big question now is who won the big game? I have no doubt that it was Phila, but I'd still like to know how bad. I guess I was paying too much attention to you there at the game to see what was going on.

   Did you have turkey for Thanksgiving? I'm enclosing a menu of what we had and we did have all that. I ate enough to last till next year, same time. I was pretty busy eating there when I heard someone say behind me "how's the food?" I said "pretty darned good" and turned around to see who it was. Here it was the new colonel, commanding officer of the field. He seems like a mighty swell fellow. He

98

*was with the Flying Tigers in China, and he'll do a lot
more for this field than the other one who's never been
overseas.*

*I saw a good show tonight. Dennis Morgan in "The
Very Thought of You". It was darned good. Bob Hope is on
Sunday in "The Princess and the Pirate". That's going to
be another good one.*

*I was wrong about those crew pictures. Actually it's
individual pictures. I don't know if our pilot has seen about
them yet or not.*

*Haven't you found out what color hair you have yet? I
guess I'm not much help but I said I'm color blind so it's
beyond me. I couldn't even say what color Mom's is. The
only way I know to describe it is a blonde brunette with a
reddish tint. Does that help any?*

*It's all right for a woman to work now in war time, but
in normal times I don't think it's right. Then the woman's
place is in the home, taking care of the kids.*

*So you got a new coat. Remember how we went to the
show in the rain and the water off the umbrella spotted
your coat. I said when it dried it would be all right. Oh
well, you can't be right all the time.*

*I don't know if I could handle the job of keeping you
warm or not but it would be nice trying.*

*I don't believe I ever did give you a name card. They're
stuck away in one of my bureau drawers at home
somewhere.*

*152 isn't such a good score. This expert that was here
when the alley opened said 160 was the average bowler's
score. Over 160 would be good. I haven't bowled for quite
a while, either. After that 88 game I bowled I sure won't
brag about my bowling.*

*I'm getting so sleepy, honey, I can hardly keep my eyes
open. So till tomorrow, sweet, good night, I love you, so
very much, in fact very, very much.*

Love forever
Dick

ARMY AIR BASE
CASPER, WYOMING

Nov. 26, 1944
9:30 A.M.

My Darling Anna:

For once I'm writing early in the morning instead of late at night. We're supposed to fly this afternoon only I hope we don't. Bob Hope is on at the show today and if we fly that means we'll miss the show, and I really want to see it. I missed one good show this week on account of flying and I don't want to miss this one.

I didn't hear from you yesterday so I have no letter to answer. I'm anxious to hear how the big game come out. Ohio State won yesterday for an undefeated season. I won $2 on that game. A couple boys in the barracks from Michigan were silly enough to think they'd beat Ohio State.

We only have a few more days here at Casper, unless they hold our class over a couple weeks and I can just see them doing that.

It didn't snow long enough here. It's cleared up already and clear as a bell. That's what I expected though. The days we don't fly it's clouded up and when we fly it's clear. It's plenty cold out though.

Have you given up smoking yet? Or have you taken up smoking a pipe? I rolled my own for a couple days, but they got some good cigarettes in now for a little while. I guess when we get to Topeka we can get all the cigarettes we want by the carton.

I guess there's not much to write about, honey, so I'll close for now. You know something, I love you just as much this early in the morning as I do in the evening. That's not surprising though, for I love you so much I can't think of anyone else, day or night. So long, darling, write soon.

Love always
Dick

Nov. 27, 1944
6:00 P.M.

My Dearest Anna:
I got to see Bob Hope after all. We flew yesterday and so I missed it then. I thought maybe I'd have some kind of ground school scheduled for today but I didn't. So I saw it this afternoon and I'm glad I didn't miss it. That Hope guy is really good. "The Princess and the Pirate" is the name of the show. The ending is really a surprise.

They have some kind of magical show tonight. It's by General Electric and they do all kind of tricks with electricity.

We fly tomorrow morning for probably the last time. It's the last scheduled time anyway.

I heard from you today. The first in about three days. It was post marked the 23rd. That's four days to get here. So you can see the mail system isn't as it should be.

We had to take off all our Air Corps shoulder patches today. They were supposed to be taken off last week but I didn't do it. The Sergeant come through the barracks today with a razor blade and took them off. We can't ship with the patches on and when we get overseas we'll get different ones anyway.

It was just a year ago today that I was hooked. I remember how I come in the Union there so happy that it was Pvt. Moore. At last I was getting away from that dead town. One year later, I'm wishing I were back in that good old dead town. It don't seem dead now when I have you to go out with.

Why shouldn't I like you wearing glasses? My love for you couldn't possibly be affected by that. I didn't think you would be near-sighted though. I'll bet you look pretty good with glasses.

Phila. must have had a tough time with Dover. You never can tell how the Thanksgiving game will turn out. Two touchdowns aren't much, but as long as it's enough to win that's all that matters.

I heard from Gene today. He sent me a couple French Francs. I guess they're not worth much in American money. He said he got a five-day pass and flew to England. That's pretty good. He said he's been flying quite a bit lately.

It won't be long before I'll know if I'll get home or not. We'll probably be leaving Casper before you even get this letter. I'm positive we won't get a furlough out of here. I hope I'll be seeing you before long though.

I guess I've run down for now, darling. All except to tell you how much I love you. I do love you, Anna, with all my heart. Good night and pleasant dreams.

Love forever

Dick

Nov. 28, 1944
11:00 P.M.

My Darling Anna:

Well, honey, I've survived Casper. After 2 1/2 months in these beat-up 24s here I'm safe and sound. I'm bound to survive combat now.

I guess we ship out about Friday. We have graduation exercises Thursday evening.

We flew for our last time this morning. We finished up our formation flying and camera gunnery. We did the camera gunnery first and then landed. Then we had a big 26 ship formation take-off. We circled the field a couple times and landed again. They have a lot of big shots here to see how good we are in formation flying. If they weren't satisfied with the formation we flew today they're crazy. Everyone was in there practically wing tip to wing tip.

I got a big Xmas box today. Kind of early but I knew it was coming. It was from the Ladel. I had a letter from them last week saying they were mailing boxes to all former employees in the service.

It was a pretty nice box. It had a small fruit cake, a package of figs, 3 handkerchiefs, a sack of candy, razor blades, shaving cream, a wallet, a deck of cards and of all things a hunk of salami.

I went to the show tonight. And it was a stinker deluxe. It was "Brazil". The only good actor was Roy Rogers who was in it a couple minutes as guest star. It was a Republic picture, need I say more.

What gives you the idea your letters aren't interesting. I could never write such swell letters as you if I tried for 50 years. I don't know what I'd do without your letters.

You must have rumor troubles too. I hope your pictures are ready pretty soon. I think we're going to have our pictures made tomorrow. We'll have the crew pictures taken in Topeka, at least that's what we're figuring on.

Please don't ever tell me to look for another girl. I'd probably shoot myself in a case like that. You're the only girl for me now and you always will be. There can be no other.

You think the Philly weather is bad, I'll bet it's warm compared to this Wyoming excuse for weather. It's really cold tonight and today we flew low altitude all the time and I still was freezing. I'm glad we're through flying here. We'll probably go to Europe though where it's just as cold.

I wrote a couple times to the girl in Dennison, but I haven't heard from her for a long time though. I don't care, for I never knew what to write to her. She probably thought I wasn't much of a writer and quit writing.

Who is this guy you've been writing to for so long? It isn't that dope named Moore is it? You should write to him often for I've heard from a good source that he loves you. Since he and I are pretty well acquainted I don't mind how often you write him.

I don't know yet if I get to go home, but I'll tell you, if you don't see me within the next couple weeks, well, you probably won't for quite a while. I'm hoping to see you soon though.

I'll close now till tomorrow, my darling. I've said it before and I'll keep on saying it forever – I love you, Anna and always will. Good night, sweet and –

Love Forever

Dick

104

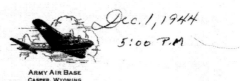

ARMY AIR BASE
CASPER. WYOMING

My Darling Anna:

Today's the day we leave good old Casper. (Good for nothing). We're still waiting for our train. I don't suppose we'll leave till late tonight. We go out on the train the new class comes in on, and so far they haven't arrived.

I just come from the show a little while ago. "Laura" was on. It was a darned good show. Gene Tierney and Dana Andrews were in it. It was a mystery and as I said before it was really good.

So they think you look pretty nice with glasses, well, I'll have to get home to see just how nice you look. Of course, I think you're mighty nice looking without glasses, but I've never seen you otherwise. I'm positive you look mighty sweet in them though.

Of course I never noticed how long (or short) as the case may be, that you wore your skirts. I never notice anything like that. What do you think I am a wolf (woof, woof)?

I'm sure I wasn't flying around the stadium on Thanksgiving. I was flying, but nowhere near Phila. I'm afraid we'd never make it and back with our gas load or otherwise I might have tried to talk the pilot into heading that way.

If there is a plane heading toward your home, they'll let you ride it when you have a furlough. Only I never have such luck.

That was Clarence Uptigraph that dropped the note in his backyard. I remember him doing it too. It was right before he went across. If I ever get over Phila. I'll drop you a note. Do you think I could hit the backyard though? (If I ever got over Phila. I'd bail out myself instead of tossing out a note.)

I guess I'd better close now darling and eat supper. Remember always that I love you and I hope that I'll see you soon (hope, I hope). So long, sweet.

Love forever,

Dick

P.S. I sent a card with my new address but in case you don't get it here it is again.

CPL. Richard B. Moore
A.S.N. 35922674
272nd AAF B.U. Sec. K.
Topeka AAF
Pauline, Kansas

CHAPTER 7
Topeka Army Air Field, Kansas

On December 3rd, Grandpa reported to Topeka Army Air Field for staging and overseas assignment.

Cpl. Richard B. Moore
A.S.N. 35922674
Gen. Delivery c/o Base P.O.
CA-11-30 Prov. Grp.
T.A.A.F.
Topeka, Kansas

> *Miss Anna Wyatt*
> *208 St. Clair Ave. S.W.*
> *New Philadelphia*
> *Ohio*

Dec. 4, 1944
11:30 P.M.

UNITED STATES ARMY AIR FORCE

Dec. 4, 1944
11:30 P.M.

My Darling Anna:
    I've finally got a chance to write. From snow in Wyoming to rain in Kansas. It's been raining ever since we hit Topeka.

The way things look, honey, I don't think I'll be seeing you this month or the next few months. In fact, the way they told us I may be across the pond within a couple weeks. I won't give up hope of getting home till I'm on the boat though.

We left Casper Friday evening and didn't get here till yesterday afternoon. It was sure a slow train ride. I'll take flying anytime.

Part of our class gets planes to fly across, part will get boats. We're in the bunch that get the boat. I can smell that old banana boat now.

They told us here that we'd all have our crew pictures taken before we left for nothing and we each get three prints of it.

All we do here is get all our records straight and get our necessary clothing and flying equipment. I think if I get as much as a three-day pass I'll head for home.

This is a pretty nice camp. They aren't quite as chicken s--- as others I've been at. The chow is plenty good. The P.X. is well stocked with cigarettes too.

I wouldn't mind getting a plane out of here. I don't like the idea of a boat. These planes here are new and good. You don't have to be afraid of them falling apart on takeoff.

I've been trying to find some of my old gang I split up with at Lincoln. They should be here but so far I haven't found them.

We've got some crew, no foolin'. The bombardier and co-pilot's been drunk ever since we left Casper.

It's getting pretty late darling, so I'd better sign off. I'll write again tomorrow. Anna, I've told you a hundred or more times that I love you and I meant it every time. I always will love you, never forget it. Good night sweetheart and write soon.

Love forever and ever
Dick

P.S. The picture is the one taken for our passes at Casper. It's guaranteed to scare hell out of anyone, including Frankenstein.

On December 6th, 1944, Grandpa left Topeka, Kansas for Langley Field in Virginia arriving on December 8th. He reported to Langley for Radar training instead of getting sent overseas.

While the Battle of the Bulge raged in Ardennes until the time of the defeat of the Germans, Grandpa was at home on furlough from December 22nd to January 2nd. He then received an Emergency Furlough from January 15th to January 22nd.

CHAPTER 8
Hope Chest

My Grandma talks about her hope chest in one of her few saved letters to my Grandpa in 1946. I have seen this hope chest in my Grandparents' attic resting at the top of the stairs for all the years that I can remember. In 2011, I asked my mom, who was in possession of the chest, if I could have it. I was always in love with it, even before I read my Grandma's letters and knew the story behind it. There was something about the inlay, the color of the wood, and the smell of cedar that engulfed you every time you opened the lid. To my surprise, my mom said yes. I am very grateful that she gave it to me, since I had assumed she wouldn't want to give up such a beautiful chest with a close connection to her mother.

After bringing it into my new home, I proceeded to clean the dust off, removed the Lubbock Army Air Field blue table covering with gold fringe that my Grandpa had brought home from his days of training there and had been kept in the chest for years. Then I pulled out the yellow-edged paper lining, stained by time, that was laying on the bottom of the chest. After I removed it, I noticed three items resting there on the bottom. I immediately recognized the writing on the two envelopes and felt my excitement start to grow. They were two lost letters that must have slid underneath the paper sometime after 1946, when my Grandma had stored my Grandpa's letters in there. All those years they were lost underneath that paper, if they were ever even missed, and I had been the one to finally find them again 65 years later. It felt a little bit like finding pieces to a puzzle or something straight out of a mystery. Clues to their story that had been hidden all this time.

The third item was a post card from my Grandma's Uncle, Tommy Curran, who was serving as a paratrooper in the US Army. At the time, he was training at Camp Crowder in Missouri, and the post card was addressed to both my Grandma and her sister Mary. With a short note saying that he was "busy as hell" and would write a letter soon. I was also extremely happy to find this because there is a photograph of Grandma posing with Tommy dressed as a paratrooper that I had always liked. And, out of curiousity, I had recently been trying to track down which company Tommy had served in. Now with this newly discovered post card, I had a new lead in my search. I now have a Camp that he had trained at and some numbers of the group he belonged too. If only he hadn't written in pencil with sloppy handwriting, I could have a much clearer view of the details. So the search for more details about his service can continue with this new information, which I can't wait to see what it leads to.

Tommy Curran (Paratrooper), Grandma, and Johnny Curran. I don't know who the man is that is standing behind them. Tommy and Johnny were Grandma's uncles.

So this is the first of the two letters that I found buried at the bottom of my treasured chest. Both letters will now be returned to their rightful resting place with the others that are stored in my Grandpa's purple flower box.

Cpl. Richard B. Moore
A.S.N. 35922674
3539th AAFBU
Sqdn. H Shellbank
Langley Field, Va.

Miss Anna Wyatt
208 St. Clair Ave. S.W.

Jan. 26, 1945
6:30 P.M.

My Very Dearest Anna,

You'll have to excuse the pencil, but we're here waiting to see if we'll fly and I didn't want to bring my pen for it leaks at altitude.

I got over to mail call right away this morning, and your picture was there. Thanks a million, darling, it's really swell. In fact, I'd say it is magnificent. That room of ours is a million times brighter now. The crew likes it too, in fact, if they'd make much more fuss over it I might even get a little jealous and hide it for fear they'll fall in love with you. It's not hard to fall for you, either, ask Dick Moore, he fell completely, head over heels.

Well, that was a quick flight, they had us sweep up the briefing rooms and take off –take off to the barracks. I can finish this letter in the peace and quiet of our little room now.

I had a letter from you also. It was only a little over a week old, but still worth reading. It was the letter telling about your pocket book being stolen. I think a person who steals is pretty low. That's one thing the Army doesn't put up with. It goes pretty hard on anyone caught stealing.

So you're going to marry me for my money, huh. You'll be mighty disappointed because that bank account's gone down again. I'm afraid it will go down further if we don't start getting paid regular. No fooling, I was further ahead as far as money is concerned when I was a Pvt. Of course, I have a good many war bonds, but ten years is a long time to wait. When I go overseas I'm going to have an allotment made out sending so much home each month. There's not

114

much to spend money for over there and we'll make more, so I should save quite a bit.

If you'd bet that I write more to Mom than I do to you or even as much, you'd lose that bet. I write to you more than everyone else put together. Spencer said I must be in love to write so often. He often goes two or three days without writing. He's right, though about my being in love. I'm very much so.

I had another surprise at mail call today. There was a letter from some girl in Magnolia who saw my picture in the paper. The letter went to Lincoln, Casper, Topeka and here, it sure got around. It was written Dec. 26. She gave her description and wants me to write. I doubt if I will though. She said she's 5'8" tall and weighs 140 lb and is 16 years old. She works in a tile plant at East Sparta. She's quite a girl for her age, I'd say.

I also had a letter from Sgt. Goudy. He wanted to know if I knew any girls down here or if I was strictly a one-woman man. As much as I talk about you when I write to him he should know better than to even ask that. I'll have to set that Sgt. straight. There is but one girl for me and you know who that is, darling.

I guess they're determined not to let me out of K.P. since I wasn't here Thursday when I was listed. I'm on Sunday's list. Actually combat crews are not supposed to pull K.P., that's why before we could go late and take off for a couple hours during the day and get away with it. But now they've found a way to get around that, they've got some pretty slick customers around this place. The night before you go on K. P. you have to report to the colonel and he gives you a direct order to go on K.P. the next day and to be there all day. Then if you don't it's too bad for you because you're disobeying his order. You can be busted to a Pvt. for that. Then they have an empty barracks where you have to sleep that night where you can be found

115

when it's time to get up. That's the height of chicken shit, believe me, now you can see what I mean when I say this place is getting worse all the time.

Another thing they come out with is that K.P. and details come before flying. If you're scheduled to fly and have K.P. or are on a detail, the work comes first, to hell with the flying. At Casper, if you were scheduled to fly, you flew regardless of whatever else you had to do. Being on a combat crew used to be a good deal, but now you're just a bunch of dogs. I guess they're using psychology here. They make you so damned mad and discouraged here that you are glad to go to combat. I know that's the way I feel now, I'd just as soon be over there where you're treated like men than be taking all the crap they shove at you in this hole.

They told us at roll call this morning that the ground school will be lengthened by four weeks which means that this training will take a month longer than originally planned.

They also told us there's a good chance of us being sent to Europe instead of China. Of course by the time we finish things may have changed again, so I don't know now where I will be sent when the time comes. I'd rather go to Europe for the Chinese theater you have to stay at least a year before being sent back, and in Europe you can finish your missions in 6 or 7 months. It just means that much sooner that I'm back in the states and back to you.

We'll get to sleep a little longer in the morning tomorrow. Since we were scheduled to fly this evening we don't have to stand morning roll call. We have beer bottles and a hammer here and if anyone tries to invade the privacy of our little room in the morning merely to wake us up, it will just be T.S. for them.

I guess I'm pretty well run down for now, sweetheart. I guess I'd better close till tomorrow.

116

I can't close without telling you how much I love you, though. I do love you, Anna darling, above all else. You're tops, sweet, and I miss you so dog-goned much. Goodnight, sweetheart, pleasant dreams.

Love forever and ever,
Dick

CHAPTER 9
Langley Army Air Field, Virginia
Radar Training

Jan. 31, 1945
7:30 A.M.

My Very Dearest Anna:
So you think you're the only one who can break resolutions, eh? Well, I guess I can too, anyway, I did. But I assure you, darling, it wasn't my fault I didn't get to write yesterday. It was quite a full day. I went to ground school all morning and afternoon, then went to fly after supper. We just landed about three hours ago. So you see I couldn't even squeeze in enough time to drop a line. I haven't been to bed for 24 hours now, almost on the dot. It was just this time yesterday morning I was crawling out of the sack. Yet I'm not the least bit sleepy right now. So now's the time to write, I guess. We're scheduled to stand by to fly again tonight. When you stand by you usually don't fly. So if we don't fly I'll answer those letters I expect to get from you

today, I hope. I didn't hear from you yesterday, that's why I expect today.

We had quite a flight tonight we took off at 9 and landed 4:30 this morning. We flew to Jacksonville, Florida and back. It would have been much better if we had flown that way in the day time when we could see the sights. Then to top things off this mission doesn't count. It was a navigation mission and our navigator's watch was running fast so his calculations weren't correct and the whole thing has to be done over.

It was almost as cold up there as it was at Casper. The heaters in the ship weren't working either, so I almost froze. It was a lot different from our first flight here. That time the ship was so warm we didn't even need the heavy clothes.

You know that heavy jacket of mine, well it's air conditioned now. I went to zip it up after we'd taken off and there at one pocket it had a nice square rip almost taking the pocket clear out. I'll have to go over and trade it in for a new one today sometime. I must have caught it on something in the bomb bay on the take off.

You remember how much I griped and complained about having to pull details and K.P., well you should have seen what happened yesterday. They put about 50 officers on detail moving big heavy wooden bins from one hanger to another. Actually, I don't see how they get away with things like that. Officers are not supposed to be put on any sort of work detail like that, but they sure were yesterday. If they pull that sort of stuff too often there will be trouble. Yet, we complain and holler about it, but what can we do, we just have to do as they tell us and like it. Well, maybe not like it, just lump it, I guess.

Today's payday, but not for Moore. The payroll was signed while I was home so I missed out on it. Now I'll have to wait till the middle or the end of next month. When

*I do get it though, I'll have quite a bit coming. I should
have two months regular pay and 3 months flight pay. That
should bring my bank account up again.*

*It's getting close to time for inspection, sweet and this
room of ours needs cleaned up a little so maybe I'd better
sign off and do it. Everyone else is asleep so it looks as
though I'm elected. The main reason I wrote now was to
tell you I love you. I do love you, Anna, and that's straight
from the heart, no kidding about it. So long till this evening.*

Love Always,
Dick

Jan. 31, 1945
3:00 P.M.

My Very Dearest Anna:
*Here I am again. I told you I would get a letter to
answer this afternoon. I didn't get much sleep this morning.
I just lay on the bed about 10 to noon and then went to mail
call. So you see a letter from you is far more important
than sleep to me. I sure hope we don't fly tonight for we're
scheduled for classes all afternoon tomorrow and that will
mean little sleep again in the morning. Oh well, too much
of your life is wasted sleeping anyway, it's just as well to
stay awake and enjoy as much of it as you can.*

*Seeing as how it doesn't happen often and after the
wonderful letter I got from you this morning, I'll forgive
you this time for not writing for two days. I hope it doesn't
happen very often. If I only heard from you two or three
times a week my morale would go down. I hope you'll
forgive me too for not writing yesterday. It won't happen
too often, I assure you, but with days like yesterday it's just
impossible to write.*

121

Maybe the reason you did bad in your bowling was because you hadn't bowled for a while. I know I'd probably roll an 88 if I bowled now, I haven't been bowling since we went the last time. It is disgusting to only get a couple pins after a spare. That's what brings the score down a lot. It takes a lot of practice to be a good bowler though. It's not a game that can be mastered after a few nights playing.

So Red did have a reason for not seeing Boots. It seemed funny that he just stopped seeing her so sudden. It all depends on how much Boots liked this guy whether he had a right to be or not. I never minded you writing to Bradford or any of the other fellows as long as it was just a friendly basis, but if you liked them more than just as a friend or vice versa, I'd be plenty mad.

It's not quite so bad when another fellow likes your girl as long as he stays away from her, but when the girl feels the same way about the guy, I'd say it was time to get things straightened out. If I ever found you running around with some other guy, not that I expect to, but if I did, I'm afraid he and I would tangle.

If he was bigger than me I doubt if that would matter, I'd be so damned mad size wouldn't make any difference, even if I would get the worst of it. I love you an awful lot, Anna and I'm afraid I'm inclined to be jealous when it comes to you.

But why talk about such things, where I'm concerned there can be no other girl. I can see no reason for stepping out when I have such a swell person as you for my girl friend. And if you love me as you say, I certainly won't worry about you stepping out. It's far too unpleasant a thought to even want to think about. I think if two people love one another the least they can do is trust each other. What do you think?

I know, Bill Angelini, of our crew and his girl were on the outs for a while because he accused her of going out with a sailor. She was really mad about it too, she wrote and said she'd never stepped out but if he was going to accuse her, by golly, she would go out with him. They almost broke up over it, but they've finally made up again. It was all Bill's fault, though. She merely mentioned that this sailor was home, and Bill knew she used to like him so he just come out and said he supposed she was going out with the sailor. I don't blame her in the least for getting mad. It's a wonder she ever wrote again. I'm afraid I'd be minus a girl if I accused you like that. Am I right darling?

So Jean's given up skating now that Tom's gone. I thought she'd give up liking him.

I never feel like going anywhere either now that you're not here to go along. I just can't have any fun, sometimes though, it gets so boring around camp. I'll get a pass and go to town just to get away from the Army for a little while. I've never been in town here yet but I used to get mighty fed up with the Army sometimes at Casper. I'd go out with the crew once in a while, but there's nothing in these towns to interest me. My only interest is back in New Phila.

Speaking of Casper, Spencer got a letter from Simpson, the kid who was in the crack up and grounded at Casper. He said they're closing the field when the class there now graduates. He also said they're still cracking them up right and left. He's afraid to wake up in the morning for fear there will be a 24 in his sack with him. I don't see why they built a field at Casper in the first place. It's the worst conditions for flying I've ever seen. They said when we got there after flying at Casper for 2 months we'd be ready for any combat flying conditions and I believe it.

So you're good at darning socks? That's more than I can say for myself, in fact, I do such a poor job of darning, I always throw them away when they get holes in them. But since you're a good darner I'll bring them to you to fix. I'm afraid you'll have to do all the sewing in our family as you could see for yourself by the job I did on my shoulder patch. I just wasn't cut out to be a house wife I guess. About the only thing I learned in the Army that's useful as far as house keeping is concerned is how to make up a sack and when I'm home I never make my own bed anyway so this Army hasn't done much good for me in that respect.

The only time I ever cared for assemblies was when they got me out of classes I didn't like. Some of those speakers they had were awfully boring. You're right, it won't be long till you're out of school. I wish I were getting out of the Army about the same time or even sooner. But chances of that don't look so good. Do you have any idea yet what you'll do after graduating?

I didn't know so many people knew me at school. I didn't hear what those girls were saying while I was talking to Miss Beaber. I don't know if I would have been embarrassed though.

I guess I'd better close for now, sweetheart, it's time for supper and then report to the line. I hope we don't fly this evening though. I feel cold just thinking about it. I'll probably have time tomorrow to write too, I just hope I hear from you. I love you so much, darling. I'm the lucky one to have such an adorable girl friend. I've still never been able to figure out how I deserve someone like you. I'll bet there's plenty of guys who envy me, but I don't envy anyone for no one else has a girl friend that can compare with you. So long for now, honey and again I love you very, very much.

Love forever,
Dick

My Very Dearest Anna:

I suppose this will be short but there's not much news right now, but I did want to write if only to tell you I love you.

Today being Sunday it was sleeping day. I didn't get up till eleven. I thought it was cold last evening in the barracks but this morning it was really cold. I hated to crawl out of that sack, but I finally got up the nerve to do it. I thought it must really be cold outside, but to my surprise it was nice out, warmer than inside the barracks.

We were scheduled to stand by for flying tonight but the weather closed in and it's now raining so all flights were cancelled. Tomorrow we're scheduled again for an 8-hour navigation mission. I don't intend flying though unless I have to. Not until I'm over this cold I have. I wish they'd schedule us for some day time flying, it's a lot better when you can see what you're flying over.

I went to see Della's sister this afternoon. I was there quite a while talking over old times and all about Phila. It's nice to know someone like that down here, when you get tired sticking around camp or have time off, I can just go visit them. She likes Langley about as well as I do.

I guess we're not going to Mulberry tomorrow as the rumor had it. I suppose they'll wait till Mom's down here and then decide to send us out.

Darling, I don't know what's wrong with me tonight. I just can't seem to write, I'm so tired and sleepy. I think it's this cold that's doing it. I'm going on sick call tomorrow, I believe and get something for it. This is sure a poor excuse for a letter, but I think I'll sign off and write again tomorrow. I'm terribly sorry it's so short, sweet, am I forgiven this time?

You know though, Anna that I love you, more than I ever have or ever could love anyone else. And I miss you so much – so dog-goned much it's practically unbearable. Darling- you're wonderful, it's no small wonder I love you so much. Good night, sweetheart, pleasant dreams and I'll be thinking of you.

Love forever and ever
Dick

After a flight at Langley Field in Februrary 1945 – Avery, Steppe, Reed, Noonan, and Randolf.

Feb. 9, 1945
9:30 P.M.

My Very Dearest Anna:
    My Brown Eyes, here I am after a hard days K.P. Well, not really hard but I did do a little more work than usual.

Evidently they're trying to make us happy here for they've now got in the mess hall, of all things, a juke box. They brought it in tonight just as we were finishing up. Personally I think they got it in the wrong building. It's the first time I've even heard of a juke box in a mess hall. Frankly it will do no good for I won't enjoy K.P. one single bit better even with music.

I suppose the mess sergeant will drop a nickel in after the meal and say, "All right boys, pick up those mops and get in the swing of this tune". Then "Ac-cent-chuate the Positive" will play and everyone starts jitterbugging with the mops. Probably though for mopping they'll play a rhumba, so you can get that hip action into it. Honestly, darling, I'm really not as crazy as I sound. You've admitted yourself that I'm crazy, but I'm not hopeless am I.

We'll have a busy day tomorrow. Ground school all morning and flying in the afternoon. If Mom is here by tomorrow I won't fly. I'll just get my pass and take off for town, but otherwise I'll fly. We'll be down by 6:30 and that suits me fine. No more of these long night flights for me.

You know why I'm in such a good humor after K.P. (I am in a good mood tonight). The reason is a very wonderful letter from you. When I hear from you I can't get mad at anything or anyone.

What's that Dover team got that we can't beat them? I suppose that's our last game with them so there won't be a chance to beat them. I doubt if the referees would cheat for Dover, they're usually pretty honest, but there's always the chance they might. That's one thing I'd hate to be, a referee or umpire, you're always accused of cheating for the other side. Would you have cussed the referee out loud? I'm only kidding, I know you wouldn't do that.

I don't think Mom being here will interfere with my writing to you. I'll write during the day then but you can be sure I'll write. How does the mail come through, anyway?

Your letters come through good now, it takes two days and they come just as regular as clockwork, except once in a while when they don't get it sorted in time.

I remember the night you fell down. I couldn't help laughing when you fell- not once but twice. It's too bad I didn't fall and give you the pleasure of laughing back. You would have had the chance if you'd seen me one night when I was coming down to your house and I went to slide down the hill. I hit the bottom and my feet went from under me so pretty. But you didn't see me so you don't have the laugh on that one.

Usually this barracks is so cold it's unbearable, tonight it's the opposite, it's too damned hot. The reason is because it's so warm outside. Tonight is just like a nice spring night back home. It seems funny to be having such nice weather this time of the year, especially after Casper.

It looks as though Bill, our tail gunner (the ladies man) is finally getting his furlough. He's supposed to get it tomorrow if nothing else turns up. I hope he does for he's been disappointed so often and he's the only one on the crew who hasn't had his yet. I know how much a furlough means too. The only trouble is in Bill's case, he lives in Massachusetts and his girl lives in Michigan, he met her while he was in the Army. He gets 10 days and it's only fair to his family that he sees them yet it wouldn't be right not to see his girl. And he's going to waste time traveling to Mass. then to Michigan. It's quite a disadvantage to live so far from your girl friend, but I guess when you meet someone and fall for them in a big way, distance means nothing. It's the same way with Spencer. He lives in Indiana and his girl lives in St. Louis. Me, I'll stick to the old home town for I have the most wonderful girl in the world there.

I guess the K.P. is beginning to tell on me for I'm getting awfully sleepy. I'd better close for now, sweet before I do fall asleep. I just want to tell you darling that I love you very much. How much? More than anyone else in the world. Why? Because you're the sweetest and most wonderful person in this world. Good night, brown eyes, I'll be thinking of you as always and pleasant dreams.

Love forever
Dick

Feb. 19, 1945
3:00 P.M.

My Very Dearest Anna:
  Sweetheart, I'm a terrible boyfriend, I missed writing again yesterday. And here I receive two wonderful letters from you today. But yesterday was an especially busy day for a Sunday. I was out at Buckroe till noon when I come in to fly, when we landed I just had time to meet Mom and we went to the show. When I left them it was so late and I was so sleepy I just had to hit the sack. I'll get back to normal again soon and write you every day, don't worry. My resolution sure went to the devil didn't it? Am I forgiven?
  We had quite a time on our flight yesterday. It only lasted an hour and a half of actual flying. We went out to bomb and had a heck of a time finding the targets. We finally picked them up and were on the bombing run when I noticed smoke coming out of No. 1 engine. I called up the pilot and told him so he stopped No. 1. After a while he started it up again and it started smoking just as bad so the pilot cut it off and we headed back for the field with three engines. We got over the field and circled for the landing. We had another fellow flying as co-pilot because Burns wasn't there. He asked Capone how long it had been since he made an emergency landing? Capone said two months ago at Casper. So the other pilot said, "Hell, it's been 7 or

129

8 months since I made one, let me try this one, Capone".
About that time we begin to sweat, but he made a good
landing.

It's not really too bad making a three-engine landing,
we had to do it at Casper purposely. But if more than one
goes on the blink that's the time to start praying.

It's a funny feeling to look out there and see one engine
stopped and that prop stock still. It wouldn't be so funny to
see three of them that way. Then it would be time to start
hooking on that chute and look for the nearest exit.

Spencer was up in the nose turret while this was going
on. He looked back and saw the engine and broke all speed
records getting from his turret back to the waist.

I've told you how the mail service was here. It's very
seldom that I forget to mail a letter. I'm positive that they
don't send mail out on Sunday from here for practically
every instance you've told me of it happening they were
mailed on Monday. Occasionally I give the letter to one of
the crew to mail when they go by the mail room but I don't
like to do it for I'm afraid they'll forget. I'll admit I am
absent-minded in some things but I always mail my letters.

I saw that card that Mom sent you, in fact, I put the
number of your house on for her, she didn't know it. How
did you like the cartoon on it?

So now you're having nice warm sunny days, well the
situation's reversed then for we're having a cold spell right
now. I'll bet the boys will have a nice cold time of it when
they fly tonight. Too cold for me, I almost froze on that
night flight I made and I want no more of it.

I'll learn to swim some day. Someday when I have the
time, then I'll learn to do a lot of things I didn't when I had
the time. I'd like to have you for an instructor, though. I
was under the impression you could swim pretty good so
don't tell me you can't swim good. It's a date, we'll go and
spend a whole day at an amusement park and surely we

130

*can find a bigger one than Youngstown. That's not far
enough to go. I wasn't wandering how to get there for we
will go in my car. I'm not only planning on having one, I
intend on having one. All the traveling I've done on trains I
see how nice a car is when you want to go anywhere. Of
course, there's the little matter of knowing how to drive
first, but that should be a simple matter. If you haven't
learned how by the time I have the car, I'll teach you how
and then we can both take the car when we want it. What
kind of car do we want? Do you like a convertible or would
you rather have a larger car?*

*I'll have to stay in tomorrow night for I'm on K.P.
again Wednesday "d--- it". Oh well, it's been close to two
weeks since the last time, I can't complain too much.*

*I guess I'd better sign off for now, sweet. I'll answer
your other letter tomorrow, I'll do my level best to get back
on the ball writing to you. You know, darling, I love you so
dog-goned much it isn't funny. In fact, I'm very serious, no
kidding about it. Why do I love you? I guess it's because
you're so darned sweet I couldn't help myself. There's a
million reasons why I love you, and they all add up to the
fact that you're tops. Good night, brown eyes, I miss you,
more than you know.*

*Love always,
Dick*

*Feb. 28, 1945
9:30 P.M.*

My Very Dearest Anna:
*I missed another day of writing, honey but I think it's
the last. From now on I can get back to normal letter
writing for I'll have more time.*

I intended writing last night but I had a heck of a surprise. I was checking the bulletin board and quite by accident I glanced at the K.P. roster for today and darned if I wasn't on it. Since I was on last Wed. I never expected it again so soon. So that upset my plans.

I only worked K.P. this morning. Capone got me off at noon so I could spend this last day with Mom. Bill Angelini took my place so I'll have to work a half day for him when he's on.

Mom's furlough ends tomorrow morning. I have to leave for camp before she goes though so I won't see her for long in the morning. Since the Colonel is back they started up this damned roll call again or otherwise I wouldn't have to be at camp till two. I'm glad they waited till Mom's stay was up or I wouldn't have had nearly as much time with her as I did.

I'm a rich man today. It's pay day and I had plenty coming. I drew over a hundred bucks. I finally got that back flying pay. I give Mom some to take back and put in my account. It needs a transfusion, that's sure. We could go out and paint the town red on that couldn't we?

I have good news concerning those pictures. Spencer got them last night and the camera does work. They come out much better than expected. So he ordered several prints of them and they'll be ready next Tuesday. They're all group pictures though. The one's Spence and I took first by ourselves didn't come out.

Mom was out to the dance at the field again last night. She won the door prize, a bottle of cologne. She kidded the fellow who was handing out the numbers. She asked him if the prize was whiskey. He said if she won and it was she'd have to half up. He was right there when she opened it to see too.

I left them at the main base waiting for the town bus. I caught the Shellbank bus. We were riding along and I noticed a big transport plane warming up on the runway. I wondered what it was doing for we had been scheduled to fly and it was called off on account of the weather. An officer sitting next to me pointed to it and said "see, that plane, President Roosevelt is in it, they just landed 20 minutes ago". They were taking off again right away, so he didn't stop long. He must have just got back from the big conference, for I see in today's paper where he just arrived, only the paper said he come by boat. I was kind of surprised when he told me who was in the plane. I imagine that's the closest I'll ever get to the president.

I knew you'd be disappointed in "Hollywood Canteen", I didn't like it at all. If Hutton hadn't heard from his girl in fourteen months I don't see why he even bothered going to mail call for he surely wouldn't expect to hear from her after that long. What do you mean I'd give you up after 14 days? I'd never give you up that easy. I'd begin to wonder, I'll assure you, but I'd find out the reason. Overseas it wouldn't be so unusual but it sure will be hard if I have to wait that long between letters. They'll mean even more to me than now, and your letters mean everything to me.

You can be sure if you didn't hear from me for two weeks while I'm on this side you can be sure it won't be my fault. Even if I had both arms broke you'd hear from me if I had to write with my feet.

You know I wouldn't kid you (about some things anyway). Even with Mom here I miss those letters when I don't hear from you for a couple days. I always manage to get to mail call for that's the most important time of the day as far as I'm concerned.

You can be sure I'm not kidding when I tell you I love you. I mean that, sweet, I mean it more than you know. I'm not kidding either, when I say you're wonderful and that I miss you so darned much. Those things I don't kid about. That's straight facts and the truth.

I guess I'd better close now, honey, I'll have to get some sleep and get up early in the morning. Good night brown eyes. I love you and only you. <u>Honest.</u>

Love forever,
Dick

Grandpa used to tell me the story of how his Mom, my Great Grandma Ella, was at an Army dance with him while she was visiting. He danced with her and his buddies were like "eh Moore, who's the lady you're dancing with?" To which he responded, "That's my Mom". So Grandma Ella must have been some looker since the boys were drooling over her. Or maybe they were just teasing Grandpa. Either way, he thought it was really a funny story.

On February 28th, 1945, President Franklin D. Roosevelt returned from the wartime meeting with Prime Minister Winston Churchill and General Secretary Joseph Stalin known as the Yalta Conference. So when my Grandpa saw his plane on the runway, the President was returning from Yalta.

March 5, 1945
9:30 P.M.

My Very Dearest Anna:
 Well, honey, after 3 long days of impatient waiting mail call come through with two wonderful letters from you. I

134

mean wonderful too, they were worth waiting for. But hearing from you is always wonderful, especially now, the way things are going around this place I surely need a lot of morale boosting.

This place is getting me down honey, no fooling. I'm taking about as much as I can stand. I'll be so damned glad to leave this place even if it is overseas. I honestly think it's better overseas. In fact, I've heard many overseas returners say if they knew what they were coming back to at this hole, they'd have stayed over there in their old outfits.

There's so much difference in fields you wonder how it can be. Lubbock was swell, I never minded the Army at all there. You were treated swell and was willing to work. Casper wasn't too good but at least they had an efficient system there. Either you flew or went to ground school not both in one day. All other time was your own. K.P. and details didn't have precedence over flying and ground school for there were no such things, they wanted to teach you things that would be of value to you not make a laborer out of you.

That's enough of my griping for now, I imagine you're tiring of it.

I went to the show tonight. It was "A Tree Grows in Brooklyn". It was good but it was a serious show. There was a lot of good acting in it.

So you hate to study, do you? Why let a little thing like a hundred word spelling test worry you. As far as I can see nothing is wrong with your spelling. Economics is an awfully boring subject. As far as I'm concerned is worthless too. I don't remember what it was all about even. Who's your teacher for that? I had old man Carroll so that was all the more reason for hating it.

What do you mean have I got my watch back yet? I've had it all along. I didn't leave it to be fixed. Mine stopped for exactly the same reason as yours. It's so dirty inside it

135

can't run. I was going to leave it till he said it would be a few months till I could get it again. I figured I could get it sooner if I had it fixed here but there's no place to get it repaired around here. I was lost without it for a while but now I'm used to it. It is a lot better to have a watch though.

We get those pictures tomorrow night so you can expect them soon. We haven't taken any more yet. There hasn't been many nice days this last week, it's just rainy day after rainy day.

What size film does your camera take? Maybe sometime I'll get lucky and be in the P.X. when it comes in, but I can't promise for you have to be there right then. It doesn't last long.

Having little time to write is often a good reason for not writing for there are days when you absolutely cannot squeeze in enough time to write even a short note. Although it's not often there are days like that. I figured when I made my new year's resolution I wouldn't be able to keep it but I intended to do my best not just because it was a resolution, but because I wanted to.

You say I'll know better than to pass a colonel without saluting. I'll know better than to pass any officer. You can't tell which of them are O.K. or which ones will stop you and take your name. If it gets much worse we'll be saluting sergeants. Everybody is salute happy around here the last couple days.

I didn't realize the basketball season was so close to the end. I don't suppose Phila. stands much chance in the State Tournament but maybe they'll surprise us and give a good showing.

What training do you mean, honey? I expect to be pretty efficient at K.P. and details sometime this month, then I can get back to my old job as a gunner. It won't be long till I'm overseas I'll grant you that but I guess I'm lucky to have stayed in the states this long. I would like to see you again first but I'm afraid that's hoping for the impossible. It's not an optimistic view I know, but I'm afraid it's so. I want more than just to be with you for a week at a time. I want to be with you for good. I love you so darned much, sweetheart, surely you realize it, you're the only girl for me.

You know what, I have K.P. tomorrow, that's one reason I'm in such a griping mood tonight. It's catching me just as regular as clockwork every week.

I think I'd better sign off soon and go to the K.P. barracks for some sleep.

I just want you to know, Anna, that I love you more than anything or anyone in this world. You mean everything to me and always will. You're tops, darling, there's none better. I love you, brown eyes, and only you. Goodnight my darling, pleasant dreams.

Love forever and ever and always,
Dick

March 17, 1945
7:00 P.M.

My Very Dearest Anna:

Here it is Saturday night, sweet and a normal Saturday night for Langley Field. Everyone is restricted, no one can get their passes. Their excuse this time is that the barracks didn't pass inspection today. It's a new one, but they always have some reason for refusing passes on Saturday night, that's what's happened three weeks in a row.

I wouldn't care in the least, but I had planned on going to Buckroe to see Dessie tonight. I haven't been out to see her and Ock since Mom left and I really should. Oh well, tomorrow's another day so I may be able to go out tomorrow night.

This weekend seems to be following the usual course all the way around. I didn't hear from you today, either. That means going till Monday, (I hope not longer) without hearing from you.

Maybe we have this air mail system all wrong. They must send free mail by air and vice versa. Only one day for a letter to get to Phila, that's really traveling. I wish all the letters would go that fast – both ways.

How long is it till graduation, sweet, not much more than a couple months, is it? I'll bet you can't wait for the time to roll around. It sure is a wonderful feeling after 12 years of waiting to think the day has finally come. I know how anxious I was for graduation day, it couldn't come too soon. Right now I should have a job somewhere, if I would have stayed at Ladel this long I'd be coming along pretty well with the machinist's trade, a fairly easy job that pays good money when you really know the trade. I guess the Army sort of delayed things a little. I'll have to wait now till it's over and start right in again learning some trade. The trouble is that I haven't learned anything in the Army to be useful afterwards. After all, who's going to be using gunners after the war. The only helpful thing I have learned is a little of what makes an airplane tick, and that isn't enough to brag about. I only hope I can get a good job after the war because it's necessary to carry out all our plans, and more than anything else, I want those plans to work out.

Do you know yet what you're going to do? Whether you'll get a job or not? I remember once you're mother said she didn't want you to work, but she wanted you to stay home and look after the house.

At least you found one letter. If there was one there should be more of them. I remember drawing planes on the back of them, that's all I used to do. Anymore though, I can't draw at all. I've tried it every once in a while but I just can't seem to do it. I hope Dort finds the rest of the letters but they won't all be A- I assure you.

You certainly can't figure out this Virginia weather. Today was a scorcher and I mean it was really hot. Right now I wish it would pour down rain and cool things off a little. I slept last night without any covers on at all, and it looks as though tonight will be worse. We flew this morning and it was warm the whole flight. We didn't even need our heavy clothes. There's a swell breeze coming through the room now. It sure feels good.

I wish we'd been on that last shipping order more than ever now. Right this minute we'd be together, maybe bowling, maybe just getting ready to go out. I'll tell you the latest rumor but don't put any trust in it for I know these Langley guarantees and I don't have the slightest faith in it. The only reason I mention it is because it sounds good. There's one crew here finished ground school and flying. Their pilot filled out furlough applications for the crew because they would have nothing else to do. One of the big-shots told the pilot that it couldn't be done, but he <u>guaranteed</u> us delay-en-routes out of here. Sounds good doesn't it? I think it's a bunch of B.S. myself. Of course I won't refuse it if they give us delays. That's one thing I won't give them any trouble about.

I had K.P. yesterday. I sure hope that's the last time. It should be if we leave when we're supposed to. We should be leaving this week – I hope. We are scheduled to fly again tomorrow and that should finish us up as far as flying is concerned. When I got off K.P. and found out we flew early in the morning, I didn't even write. I took a shower, laid down and went to sleep. I was sure tired, and still am as far as that goes. We were wrestling around with a bomb at 10,000 ft. this morning and that's quite a workout.

It happened while we were bombing this morning. We made the bomb run and two bombs released instead of the usual one. Something was messed up and instead of the bottom bomb falling as it's supposed to, the one above it released bumping the bottom one as it went out and knocking it loose from half of its fastening.

You should have seen that bomb go. When it hit the other it naturally threw it off course. Instead of falling out it was thrown back spinning wildly into space. I'll bet that's the farthest Reed ever come from the target.

Well the bomb that was knocked out of place was only in the road then. It wouldn't be released in that condition. I went back and got Spence to help and when we got to the bomb bay there was our navigator with the bomb in his lap sitting across the bomb bay. We carried it up front and that's quite a job in that narrow bay. Then we had to figure out what to do with the darned thing, and decided to make another run and a couple of us hold it out and drop it by hand when Reed give us the signal. Welch, the navigator, didn't like the idea though, he was afraid one of us would go out with the bomb.

So we had to go to the trouble of hooking the bomb up again so it would release electrically. I guess Welch was right, there's not much sense taking a chance like that for nothing, even if it would be the easy way. Other than that little incident we had no trouble at all dropping the rest of them. I guess we need something to break the monotony though.

Come to think of it, it is only about two months since we last said good bye, but darling it seems so much longer, at least two years to me. Right now I'd like to be looking into those lovely brown eyes of yours and telling you I love you so much instead of being so many miles away and just writing about it. Of course writing is O.K. when it's all you can do, but I'd much rather tell you in person. It's been 15

140

months now since we first said good-bye. A lot has happened in that time. I've been falling deeper and deeper in love with you every day of those months.

I think were going to get that rain I was wishing for. It's beginning to thunder and lightning. If I get what I wish for that easy, I'll start wishing for that 18 day delay right now.

I think I'll sign off sweet. I have to write to Gene yet, it's been so long since I've written him. Oh, I forgot. Bill saw Burns in town last night and he was feeling his drinks a little so he was in a talkative mood. He told Bill that he missed us guys. Bill asked him why he got off the crew then. It's as I figured. He don't think much of Capone. He said Capone don't fly the ship, the ship flies Capone. I think he'd like to be back on the crew as pilot. I know darned well the crew wishes the same thing.

Just one more thing I haven't forgot and I hope you never forget, brown eyes. I love you, Anna, and I miss you more every day. You're so sweet and wonderful, everything a guy could ask for. I can't help but love you honey. Good night sweetheart and pleasant dreams.

Love forever and always

Dick

March 22, 1945

12:00 NOON

My Very Dearest Anna:

Here I am at the Mulberry Island range, we'll be going back soon this afternoon though. We were only out here one day, but I wish we'd been out here our whole stay at Langley Field. It's just as nice out here as everyone said it would be. No Colonel or any of his stooges to tell you your hat's on crooked or you have a hair out of place. No *chicken whatsoever. All these instructors are overseas returnees and they're really good Joes. We were only to be out here for one day so they said we couldn't get much done, so we haven't done a thing. Yesterday we played softball. This morning we slept till dinner time. And what food. It's really good compared to the chow you get at the field. And there's no such thing as K.P. here. K.P. is done by German Prisoners of war. They must be trusted or something for they have no guards at all over them. They run around the place free as the birds. Those guys are good for something it seems. I think it would be a good idea if they'd spread the idea of German K.P.'s all over the country, so there'd be no more of it for we poor corporals.*

I've got bad news though. It's pretty certain I won't get home this time. Of course, every other time I got home I didn't expect to but this time I'm positive. We're going to see sunny California. It's Salinas, California, a little below San Francisco. The thing about it is some of the crews are going to Mitchell Field, New York and they get delays. I really wish we'd been on that shipment. We'll probably be leaving Saturday or Monday. I'm really glad to be leaving Langley but darn it, honey, I wish I could have seen you again. California is a long way off.

This is pretty short, sweet, for I don't have much time right now. The buses should be coming pretty soon. I'll write again as soon as we get back to the field.

I love you brown eyes, I hope it's not too long till I see you again. So long Anna, write often, for I miss you so much.

Love forever,
Dick

CHAPTER 10
Capone's Crew

March 23, 1945
10:30 P.M.

My Very Dearest Anna:
Well, darling, I had quite a busy day. I made a discovery today. They have a golf course out in the hospital area only a ten minute ride in the bus. When we found that out the crew decided to go out and play. It's a good deal too. They furnish the golf clubs and the only cost involved is a golf ball. And once you buy that you don't have to pay anything after that.

I've never really played golf before. They only time I ever tried it was once when I was about 12, I was caddy for Gib. So you can imagine I didn't do too well. In fact, none of us did too well, we quit keeping score after the fifth hole. It's a lot of fun, add that to the list of things we have to do after the war. I'll bet you'll really enjoy the game, or have you already played it before.

We're going to ship out Monday and it is Salinas, California. And it is also definite we get no delays out of here. I didn't have much hope for it to begin with but I really wanted to get home again to see you once more before shipping over.

We lost one man off our crew, that's another thing we knew was coming but didn't want to see happen. It was a toss-up between Noonan and Angelini and Angelini lost.

143

Now he's off the crew and will stay at Langley. He'll probably be put on another crew and sent through all this training again. If I wasn't assistant engineer I might have been the one to leave. Noonan is assistant radioman so that's one reason he gets to stay on. It is a heck of a note, though. After going through all this training together, get to know the guys real well, I'm just glad it wasn't me. Bill feels pretty bad about it, but maybe he'll get a better deal than us out of the whole affair.

It may also mean that I'll be the new tail gunner, in fact, I'm pretty sure of it. I don't much care for one gun position is about the same as another.

I went to the show this evening. It was "God is My Co-Pilot". It was a good show about the Flying Tigers in China. Dennis Morgan was star and Dane Clark. Some say the name of the picture should be "God Am My Co-Pilot" but that's incorrect grammar and don't sound quite right.

I'm sorry honey, but I don't think I can quite make the spring formal as much as I'd like to. The government says they need me pretty bad out in California. They can't quite see there way clear to let me go by way of New Phila.

That's some deal when Boots introduces a friend to Red and she takes him away from Boots. What's wrong with Boots giving up without a struggle? I certainly hope you care more than that for me.

So you're thinking of going to Washington. I don't know what to tell you on that, honey. If you really think you'd like the job, I'd say go ahead. After all, if you didn't like it you could always quit. I guarantee it's a good experience for since I've been away from home I've learned quite a bit about getting along on my own hook.

You say you'd never move back to the old neighborhood if you ever moved away. I don't know, sweet, I'd sure like to be back in the same old neighborhood again. Of course, the main reason I miss St. Clair so much is not St. Clair itself, but it's a certain girl who lives on that street. If you'd be in Washington I'd want to be there too. I'd want to be with you no matter where you were darling for I miss you so very much.

Enclosed in this envelope you will find the miracle of a century. Our whole crew all together. Honey, meet the boys.

Ernie Capone – pilot, no relation to Al the gangster he claims. His main gripe in this Army is the fact that he's been a 2nd Lt. for 26 months. He should be made happy soon for he's up for promotion to First Lt. and should get that silver bar soon. He's a good pilot with a lot of flying time and I think he can pull us through any tight spots. (Hartford, Conn.)

Bob Spencer – Armorer Gunner – nose turret. 21 years old unmarried 5 ft. 4 inches of dynamite. Hot shot with the women. They all go for the little mustache he has (it's too light to show up in the picture). (South Bend, Ind.)

Walt Noonan – happily married man with one child, a cute little baby girl – Waist gunner. Walt's an ex-fuller brush salesman. He can talk his way in and out of anything. I don't see why he's in the Army at all for I'm sure he could out talk any five draft boards put together. (Hartford, Conn.)

Dick Moore – Joe Dope of the crew. Unmarried (at present). Not much good for anything. All he does is talk about a girl named Anna. He says he loves her and I believe he does and I mean he's got it bad. (New Phila. Ohio)

Bill Angelini – Ex-tail gunner. He's the one we lost off the crew today. Sometimes he was hard to get along with but all in all he was O.K. and we hate to lose him. (Fall River, Mass.)

Thornton Avery – Radioman. You figure Avery out, we can't. He has some funny ways sometimes. He'll argue for dear life over a penny. He's a good egg though, it's just that all radiomen are slightly off their nut from listening to so much static. He's married and his wife expects a baby in May. (Cleveland, Ohio)

Warren Steppe (or Squeaky). Engineer. He's my chief, the guy I'm assistant to. Steppe knows the B-24 inside out. When anything goes wrong with that box car he's the boy that fixes it. He's the rebel on the crew. He said our crews proportioned just right for one rebel can whip ten Yankees any day of the week. He's also a happy husband and father. (Columbia, South Carolina)

Bill Daley – Co-Pilot. This isn't too good a picture of Daley but I assure you he's not like the Daley of New Phila. I can't say much about him for I've only seen him a couple times since he joined the crew. He's only flown with us once. I do know he's a screwball though, crazy as the devil. He can't take Burns place though I'll tell you that. (Hartford, Conn.)

Randolph – Radar Operator (or Mickey Man). He's a pretty good egg too, but I don't know a whole lot about him. He's a close neighbor of ours though. We told him he never seen the light of day till he joined the Army. He's from Pittsburgh, Pa.

George Reed – Bombardier – This is our boy. We think more of Reed than any of the other officers. He's been with us the longest and he's really tops. He's more like a G.I. than an officer. Everyone likes Reed, he's easy to get along with and I don't believe he has an enemy in the world. He's a cowboy from Billings, Montana.

Alvin Welsh – Navigator – In the air he can find his way pretty good but on the ground he just can't navigate, he's always lost. He's always showing up for inspection with his P.T. clothes on and shows up for P.T. dressed up for inspection. (Madison, Wisc.)

That's it Anna, crew 1198, Capone's Torpedoes. We've had good times together and some pretty rough times together. Here's hoping we'll come through this war together. Knowing this crew pretty well I think they will.

Did you ever read how Elliott Roosevelt become a general through his good work with the aerial camera. If he can do it, so can I. My commission should come through any day now.

Darling, I believe I'd better close for now. We have to get up early in the morning to start processing. I'll write again tomorrow.

There's nothing more to say except that I love you so terribly much, brown eyes. I really hate the idea of shipping to California for it's taking me further away from you than I've ever been. Some day those trains are going to be heading toward Phila. instead of away and I'm just waiting for the day I'll be on that train. Good night, sweetheart, I love you and only you.

Love always,
Dick

Although I can't locate the photo that Grandpa was talking about in this letter, I have included a photo of his crew that they called "Capone's Crew" or "Capone's Torpedoes". Most of the men described in the letter, are in this photo.

Back Row: Ernest Capone (Pilot), Robert Spencer (Gunner), Walter Noonan (Gunner), Richard Moore (Gunner), Bill Angelini (Gunner), Thornton Avery (Radio Operator), Warren Steppe (Flight Engineer)
Front Row: William Daley (Co-Pilot), Donald Randolph (Radar), George Reed (Bombardier), Alvin Welch (Navigator)

Grandpa posing like Elliott Roosevelt's photograph in Feb. 1945.

Cpl. Walter F. Noonan (Waist Gunner, Asst. Radio Op.,

Asst. Engineer, Photographer) from Hartford, Connecticut.

After looking at a series of photos of Grandpa and his buddies crouched down holding aerial cameras, I asked Grandpa why they are all in that same pose. He told me that he and his crew had seen this article about Elliott Roosevelt and how he flew photographic missions. The article featured a picture of him holding an aerial camera. So they were playing around taking photos and had all of them pose the same way.

*This is the second letter that I found in my Grandma's hope chest that had been lost all those years under the paper lining.

March 25, 1945

My Very Dearest Anna:
 Tomorrow's the big day, sweetheart. We're leaving Langley. I know definitely I won't get home now and probably for a long time. At Topeka I thought I was going across then and now I think this is it. And I believe this time it's positive. I expect to be overseas in at the most a month from now. You know last night I dreamt I was home. It was the same dream. I got home on Saturday afternoon. All I could think of was " I have to see Anna. I only have tonight, we can go to a show and I can be with her tonight, but I have to be back at Langley in the morning for a 10 o'clock formation". How I could leave Phila. Saturday night and be back here Sunday morning beats me but that's the way the dream went. The only trouble was I didn't get to see you. Someone woke me up. It was Reed. He was drunk as a lord and it was seven o'clock. We chased him

150

out of the room and went back to sleep but I couldn't pick up the dream again.

We went out and played another round of golf this afternoon. I did a little better this time than last but I'm still far from even an average golfer. With a little practice I could do all right but I don't think we'll have much chance to play golf where we're going.

We're going to have quite a busy day tomorrow. Packing bags, last minute details getting ready to ship so I won't have any time for writing then. So if you don't hear from me for a week or longer you'll know the reason. We're going to be on that train for 5 or 6 days.

Why talk about the trip. Darling it may be a long time before we see one another again. But I want you to know. Every time I've said I love you- I meant it. There's no two ways about it. In my opinion Anna there's no one nearly as swell as you. The crew was talking about what's ahead of us but we all agreed on one thing. <u>We're coming back.</u> Some of the boys have wives and kids, the rest of us have someone that means a lot to us. I have you sweet, you're the girl I'm coming back to, the one who means everything to me. We've got the future ahead of us and I intend being here to see it.

We've had some good times together. At least to me it's that way. Every minute I'm with you I'm happy. Even before we actually started going together we had some swell times. Marge West and Nug never meant a thing to me. You've always been the one and only whether you knew it or not.

I'd give anything to see you once more, but there's no use talking about the impossible. There's not much more to say right now. I just want you to know you mean the world to me. I miss you brown eyes I miss you so very much. Goodnight my darling. <u>I Love You.</u>

Love forever and always,

151

Dick

In 2011, I was producing a short film for a traveling museum exhibit called *Rise Above* for the Red Tail Squadron, a non-profit organization that uses the story of the Tuskegee Airmen to help inspire kids to achieve their goals. One of our shoots brought us to Langley Air Force Base in Virginia to film the P-51 Red Tail Mustang doing its air show routine.

We were only on the base for one day and there wasn't much time to wander off and do some research. But through some inquiries to some people in the media department, I learned that the buildings and hangers we were standing around, were built in the 1930's. So there is a good chance that I was in some of the same places that Grandpa was nearly 70 years ago. Following the railroad tracks next to the roads on our drive into Langley AFB, I could imagine them as one of the railroad lines that brought Grandpa into the base when he was only a teenager. Seeing the places that he might have been does bring a whole new dimension to the stories he would tell.

I hope to return to the base someday and to have the time to research where Grandpa spent his time training and where he lived.

CHAPTER 11
Salinas Army Air Field, California
Staging

On March 26th, 1945, Grandpa headed for Salinas, California, arriving there on April 1st, where he reported for staging. Meanwhile, in the Pacific, the United States started the invasion of Okinawa. Where Grandpa would soon be heading.

Cpl. Richard B. Moore
A.S.N. 35922674
451st A.A.F.B.U. Sqdn. T.
Salinas Field
Salinas, Calif.

Miss Anna Wyatt
208 St. Clair Ave. S.W.
New Philadelphia
Ohio

April 4, 1945

My Very Dearest Anna:
Today is a special day. My mail started coming in again. It started off especially wonderful with a swell letter from you. Of course it was only written over a week ago. I'm not complaining though, a letter from you is worth a

153

million times its weight in gold, even more when it's been so long since I heard from you.

I'd sure like to see you with your new permanent. I'll bet you look mighty sweet, well, naturally – you always do. (I'd like to see you). No fooling, sweet, I really miss you. I'll bet when I get overseas all I'll do in my spare time is sit around and look at your picture and think back to the swell times we've had together. And also the better times we'll have in the future. Maybe that future of ours isn't too far off.

Speaking of the future I didn't have much faith in fortunes till the other day when I weighed myself on one of those fortune telling scales. The card said, "You will soon have an opportunity to travel, if you don't go you'll miss a thrilling adventure." What do you think, sounds like I better not miss out.

You must be having pretty warm weather back home too. I think it's about time it warmed up though after all that snow and cold weather this winter.

I guess if your Dad is teaching you to drive, you'll have to teach me. With the gasoline shortage I wouldn't be a bit surprised if the car run out of gas in a lonely spot.

I wish that film would have turned out good. I wouldn't say I had plenty of pictures of you. I could have an album full and still it wouldn't be enough. Anymore I don't even have to get your pictures from my wallet to look at them, I have them imprinted perfectly in my memory. I've nearly wore them out looking at them.

When you said there's never a dull moment on this crew of ours you weren't fooling. We had quite a time in town the other night. There were four of us together. Our engineers always telling us how he can hold his liquor. He left us for a while and when we saw him again he was drunk – really drunk. We had to be back at camp pretty soon and the bus driver wouldn't let him on. We had three *of the crew, two M.P.'s, two officers and a half dozen other guys arguing with that driver to let him on but it was no use.*

We finally got him back to camp in a taxi. When we got in the barracks he wanted to beat the devil out of some other fellow. He was in no condition to do any fighting so I had to throw him on the bed and sit on him to get him quiet. Then I talked him into going to bed. What a time, I said the next time he goes talking about how much liquor he can hold, I'll clip him. No, never a dull moment.

There's not much more to write about right now, sweet so I'd better sign off. Oh, yes, I forgot. We have more rank on the crew now with two new promotions. Capone and Reed are now first lieutenants. I guess they deserve it though after being 2nd Looies for a couple years.

Something else I didn't forget honey or never will forget. I love you, brown eyes. I do love you and I miss you so very much. I hope it's not too long till I see you again.

I'll write again next chance I get and here's hoping there's more mail tomorrow from you. Good night sweetheart and pleasant dreams.

Love always,
Dick

On April 12th, 1945, President Roosevelt passed away, only months after Grandpa had seen his plane in Langley.

April 16, 1945

My Very Dearest Anna:
I tried my luck at bowling again last night and I did a little better than the other night, (thank god). The first three games weren't too good, but the last game I rolled 152,

which for a bowler like me is good. For good bowlers that score is only average. We didn't have to set our own pins last night, maybe that's what was wrong the other night I was too wore out from setting the pins for Spence and Noonan I couldn't bowl right. Well, don't look at me like that, one excuse is as good as another.

I went to the show last night. Jack Benny was on in "The Horn Blows at Midnight". It was a screwy show, purely fantastic. All about angels and heaven. It was pretty funny in spots though.

The show tonight is "Dillinger", all about the gangster. I suppose our crew should go and get some pointers. Capone's gang, you know. We could learn some tricks of the trade.

I'm trying to talk the crew into going skating instead though. I haven't tried the rink out in town here yet. From what they say none of the rest of them can even skate that's why they won't go. It's been quite a while since I've been skating too. It was when I was home. That's only three months but it seems so much longer since I last saw you. I don't enjoy skating too much without you, but I'd better keep in practice or I'll be worse than ever next time I'm home. I doubt if there will be any roller rinks where I'm going so I'd better go when there is one around.

This place is getting more like Langley. They have us on detail again, this time cutting grass. I hear they're going to issue gunners picks and shovels as standard equipment from now on. The only trouble here is that it's too hard to get out of it. At Langley, we just wouldn't report to detail. Here they check too close and we have to be there. The only good thing here is that we don't pull K.P. – as yet. It really isn't too bad though we have it lots easier here than at Langley. We're kept busy with a lot of things but we don't have quite as much C.S. to put up with.

156

I've still had no mail from you yet. I really had hopes yesterday too. Maybe today – as I have said everyday the last two weeks.

It's about time for chow now, sweet. I supposed I'd better sign off. They have fairly good chow here considering that it's army chow. I still prefer good home cooking naturally.

You know the thing I want most of all right at this moment. A letter from the girl I love so much, namely you, brown eyes. I do love you Anna and I miss you so doggonned much, more than you know. So long for now sweetheart, I'll be thinking of you.

Love always,

Dick

Grandpa (left) and some of his buddies from April 1945.

CHAPTER 12
Mather Field, California
Overseas Processing

While German forces were surrendering, days after Hitler's suicide, Grandpa reported to Mather Field for overseas processing and instruction on May 2nd, 1945.

Cpl. R.B. Moore
A.S.N. 35922674
A.P.O. 19194-BW-8
c/o Postmaster
San Francisco, Calif.

> *Miss Anna Wyatt*
> *208 St. Clair Ave. S.W.*
> *New Philadelphia*
> *Ohio*

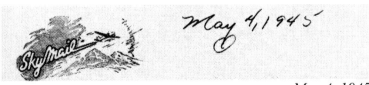

May 4, 1945

My Very Dearest Anna:
   Sweetheart, this was really my lucky day. I received four, yes I said four wonderful letters from you, all in one day. And – that's not all – also an especially wonderful

159

Easter card. It's a swell card, darling. It goes without saying those letters were welcome and I do mean welcome. They sure boosted my spirits quite a bit.

You know what, four letters calls for four answers. So I'm going to answer each and every one separately. That way I can tell you I love you that many more times.

Four days would seem to be a miracle in mail service to me. This letter I'm answering now was mailed on April 13th. I just received it today. Figure out for yourself the kind of mail service I'm getting.

So the reason I didn't hear from you for quite a while was because you didn't write. Well, darling, you know doggoned well I'll forgive you. You're so darned sweet I'd forgive you for anything – that is almost anything. You can't realize just how much I missed those letters though. If you did you'd never have stopped writing. Why the first letter I received from you at Salinas I sat right down outside the mailroom and read it through twice, that's how anxious I was to hear from you.

Darling, I don't ever feel it's a chore writing to you, something that has to be done because there's no way out of it. I'll never feel that, I write because I want to write to you. Actually I consider it a pleasure, although I know of some of the letters I write couldn't be considered a pleasure to read. The rest of the boys wanted me to go into town with them tonight, but I'd rather stay here and write to you. They've formed the opinion that I must be pretty much in love with you, and they are 100% correct.

So you admit you don't love me, that you're a gold-digger. Ah, fickle woman, you break my heart. You're heading for a downfall if you intend marrying me for money, little woman for alas- I have no money – only war bonds.

No, sweet, you'll just have to learn to love me for myself, not for my money.

So J.B. doesn't like holding hands in the hall. Tell him he's an old-fashioned fuddy duddy – even stronger names, if you care too. He's probably jealous because he can't do it himself. That rule about smoking on the school grounds has always been in effect. (Say what do you do now, sneak into the rest room and smoke) I haven't had any cigarette trouble lately, in fact since I left Casper. The rationing at Langley was a laugh. I had more cigarettes there than I could smoke.

You're not kidding darling, those spring evenings would be nice if you were here to spend them with. You'd make any evening anywhere complete.

I'll close this letter now darling. I want you to know sweet that I love you so very much. You're so sweet, I can't help but love you. I can't name one guy in this Army (or Navy either) who has a sweetheart even as half as wonderful as you. I guess that makes me the luckiest guy in the world. I won't say goodnight for I'll be with you again in a couple minutes. I love you, brown eyes.

Love forever
Dick

May 4, 1945

My Very Dearest Anna:

Here I am back again sweetheart, ready to answer No. 2 letter. This was written on the 19th about a week later than the
first, - good mail service. I remember getting the letters in between back at Salinas.

I like to sit and listen to the radio once in a while too, but there are none in the barracks here. Back at Salinas we had three of them. It was O.K. as long as they didn't have a different program on each.

I agree with you, Jack Carson is one of the best. He's got a certain type of comedy all his own. I saw "Roughly Speaking" back at Langley. It was a good picture all right, but there's not too much comedy in it. It has its bright spots, brightened, of course, by Carson.

You're complaining about cold weather and I'm complaining about hot weather. Maybe we should get together on the situation. Maybe we should get together period. That sounds like a wonderful idea to me. Tonight's the first cool night we've had since we hit this field. I've even got my jacket on for the first time since I left Salinas.

Say, Miss Wyatt, what happened to your honor student standing? I'll admit though four B's are nothing to complain about. What happened to you in typing? I know, flirting with the teacher too much.

This was the shortest letter of the four so I guess it will be a short answer.

Your picture here on the shelf in front of me made me think of something. If you only knew how many times it's been packed and unpacked and how many miles it's traveled since I've had it you'd be surprised. Just in the last week it's been packed four times only to be taken back out to occupy its place on the shelf. We've really been moving around lately.

Well brown eyes, again I'll tell you I love you. I do, sweet, there's not a doubt about it. Every time I think of how sweet and wonderful you are, I wish there was some way I could personally stop the war this very minute so we could be together again. But unfortunately, I'm not endowed with any such power so I guess we'll have to go on waiting - but darling, it's so awful lonely without you just waiting. I miss you terribly, darling and I love you so terribly much.

Love always,
Dick

162

My Very Dearest Anna:
Here goes on the third super-wonderful letter I got from you today.
You say most of my letters you got were post-marked the same day regardless of when they were written. That's the way the mail service at Salinas was messed up. That whole postal service there was a screwball affair. They told us when we got there mail was sometimes held for 48 hours. Why is beyond me, but I guess they did it.
I wouldn't say I'd never put a show before answering my mail. Certain mail I've put off for my own pleasures, but I generally do my writing before going anywhere. And I always make sure that nothing like a show stands in the way of writing to you.
I noticed in two of your letters you mentioned about cleaning the couch. I see that you keep it in good condition. I hope you do for I wouldn't want anything to happen to it. I hope to be sitting on that with you again some day, not too far from now.
I don't know about Truman making a mess of things at the peace conference. Roosevelt would let the other nations have their own way too much to be diplomatic. Truman seems to put his foot down and wants things his way. That's the only way we'll get the things we want out of the peace, maybe Truman's a better man than he was figured for.
I guess I was pretty lucky getting home so often considering the deal Ray got. He's been in a long time without a furlough. I wouldn't consider 6 or 8 months a short time either. But when you think how long he's been in it would seem a very short time with a furlough in sight.
I guess it wouldn't do any good for you to live in a town near where I was stationed unless you'd move every time I

did. I can't seem to stay in one spot very long. It ranges from four days at Topeka to four months at Langley Field. I've only been at ten different fields in 16 months. That's an average of about a month and a half at each. Maybe I can get stationed permanently at Wright Field or Lockbourne in Columbus. I'm sure I wouldn't mind staying a while at either of those fields.

Darling, sometimes the way you misunderstand me I could cuss. I wouldn't be that cheerful over receiving the Ladel paper except for the fact that I meant my mail was to come through. I was happy over the prospects of the letters from you to come, not over the stinking paper I had that day. I suppose every time I tell you how much your letters mean I'm just kidding, just beating my gums, just taking up space by making up something. No, sweetheart, I'm not kidding one bit and you know it. Your letters do mean everything to me whether you think I'm kidding or not. As much as I love you, - well it gets pretty discouraging not to get mail from you for days at a time.

I'm afraid I couldn't teach anyone much about bowling. Not at the rate I bowl anyway. In fact, I could stand quite a few lessons myself. Setting pins is definitely not fun. It's too much work for the pay. I'd never set them except the way we were. As far as doing it to earn money I'd stay broke.

Well, sweet it's time to tell you again that I love you. You're so darned lovable I couldn't help falling for you. I've been falling deeper and deeper the longer I know you too. I miss you something awful brown eyes.

Love forever and ever,
Dick

May 4, 1945

My Very Dearest Anna:

And so, sweetheart, I start to answer the fourth and last of you letters I received today. I wish I could be as lucky each and every day.

You're not the only one who's lonesome darling, I'll guarantee you that. Every time I think of the swell times we've had together and the better times we're going to have, I get a sort of empty feeling. I miss you so very much. Nothing I do is complete without you. Yes there are many in the same boat as us, and a good many not quite as lucky as us. I don't ever wonder if the war will end because I know it's bound to end someday. It just seems that it's taking an awful long time to end. Far too long. I'm getting awfully anxious to start out on those plans of ours.

I told you before that I wished we had went overseas last December when we were supposed to, well, I still wish we had. You remember Pickhardt, our first co-pilot. The last I heard of him, he had most of his missions in and will soon be coming back to the states, maybe now he's even back. That would be rough now, wouldn't it, getting back in time for your summer vacation. But why talk about things that could be, we're not quite so lucky.

I'd rather imagine you would look very nice in black. You'd undoubtedly be the belle of the prom. You will be anyway, no matter what color formal you wear. I would like to be there to be with you. Everyone would say how does that jerk rate, having the best looking girl here when he doesn't even go to school. I know I'd be the envy of every guy there.

You have the right attitude now, why study for a test, it don't pay. All studying does is confuse you. I got through school fairly well on an absolute minimum of study. You know yourself I never took books home and I spent all my study halls reading magazines.

I'd make a mighty poor lawyer. Every time I argue I contradict myself. It is hard to argue on the point of marrying young, though, there's too many points to consider.

As far as we're concerned by the time I'm back from overseas we will be old enough. One thing is sure, we won't get married till I get back, and the way I feel about you I'm figuring on it. Or am I taking too much for granted. I've been hoping that you feel the same way.

It's getting pretty late darling. I guess I'd better sign off for tonight. You know, brown eyes, at least you should by now that I love you very much. You're the only one for me and that's all there is to it. So for now, sweet, I'll say goodnight. Write often, you're letters mean so much. I love you.

Love forever and always,

Dick

In 2011, I flew into San Francisco for a television shoot that I was producing. It was for a TV series called *The Restorers*, a show about people who restore vintage aircraft. We were doing a story covering the Collings Foundation's Bomber Crew Fantasy Camp in Stockton, California. The camp was created to let people experience what it was really like for the boys who were trained to fly on the B-24 bomber. I was able to experience the camp in a vague sense, through documenting their activities and stories with the occasional participation.

On the first day, I was allowed to ride on the B-24 bomber for the trip to the Stockton Airport, to kick off the start of camp. The pilots were great guys who were wonderful enough to allow me to stand and look out of the top hatch and act as the flight engineer while we taxied down the runway. My job was to make sure that the wing tips didn't collide with anything getting too and from the runways. Standing up there, getting a view of the top of the airplane, I could just imagine Grandpa getting to do the same thing. It was one of the most amazing experiences I've ever had.

After take off, the pilots gave the ok that we were free to roam the aircraft. I was in the seat behind the pilots, so I unbuckled and squeezed through the catwalk in the bomb bay with the air and light rushing in through the closed, thin metal doors to make my way to the back of the plane. When I entered, the waist gun windows were open and I found myself standing on the edge of the ball turret below me. I looked into the large gaps surrounding it that went straight through to the earth miles below me with nothing between us but the wildly whirling air. Bright California sun was bursting through every opening and window, lighting up the tail in a soft glow. Not being a huge fan of heights, it was one of the most terrifying moment in my life.

I took a deep breath and steadied myself against the rocking airplane that could toss you around like you were on a ship in a storm. A big camera in one hand and grabbing onto whatever metal structural pieces I could find with the other, I made my swaying walk towards the tail gunner position.

I didn't have much time, so I squeezed myself into the tail gunner seat, banging my arms and legs on all sorts of metal parts along the way. It was incredibly bright from the sun and I immediately felt very warm with the glass bubble dome around my head. By the time I made it back there, I was only there for mere minutes before having to return to my seat for landing. Though it was a short amount of time, I was able to get a small sense of what it must have been

167

like for my Grandpa. While I thought to myself how bright, noisy and windy it was in there, Grandpa would have been flying at higher altitudes making it much, much colder with missions sometimes lasting for 12 or more hours. I was wearing shorts and a t-shirt under my WAC coveralls (required for our film crew to wear so that we blended in with the camp), and it was quite cold with the wind. So I can only imagine how awfully cold it would be at higher altitudes, even with the warm clothes they would wear. And being cramped in that tail gun position for hours on end, not to mention the possibility of getting shot at and potentially killed. This incredible expecience adds to my great respect for what those men and my Grandpa went through to protect our country and the world from invading forces.

Although it was a quick flight and I was filming for most of it, I did get to make a quick trip to the tail gunner position, where Grandpa had once sat. I'm eternally grateful to the pilots and to the Collings Foundation for allowing me to have that experience.

After I landed, the next part of Bomber Fantasy Camp took us to a ranch where they would fire some WWII weapons, including the M1 Garand, M1 Carbine, a German Luger, and a Colt .45. The people running the camp, were gracious enough to allow my film crew and I to fire the weapons. Shooting those guns allowed me to feel what those men had experienced, minus having someone firing back at you. They were heavy, powerful weapons that I'd hate to be on the other end of. To imagine having to lug those weapons on top of all their other gear for endless amounts of miles, while fighting for their lives, really gave me a new understanding of history.

While I had the best time getting to experience the camp, I am incredibly sad that I am not able to share this story with my Grandpa. I can just see his smile and hear his laugh in reaction to my adventures. I wish more than anything that I could see him again, just to feel the touch of his hand on mine, as he would often do, to silently show how he loved our conversations.

CHAPTER 13
Flight to the Pacific Theater

Grandpa had started to go overseas on May 6th, but had to turn back due to navigation trouble. On May 8th, 1945, Grandpa took off at 0400 for his 15 hour flight to Hawaii, as one of his first legs of travel to the Philippines.

He landed at John Rogers Field on Oahu. After Germany's unconditional surrender, victory was declared in Europe, so Grandpa and his crew celebrated V-E Day with free beer and hot dogs. He then visited Honolulu on May 9th.

On May 10th Grandpa left Oahu in the morning and stopped at Palmyra Island to refuel. After 11 hours, he landed on Canton Island in the evening.

Cpl. R.B. Moore
A.S.N. 35922674
A.P.O. 19194-BW-8
c/o Postmaster
San Francisco, Calif.
(Canton)

Miss Anna Wyatt
208 St. Clair Ave. S.W.
New Philadelphia
Ohio

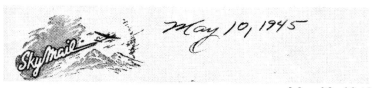

My Very Dearest Anna:
Here I am in Canton. Surprise!! No I don't mean Ohio.
I wish it were that one. It's some place, just like the
descriptions of places overseas. You know one of those one
tree places. And I'm not kidding, there is only one tree.
We're living at the Savoy Plaza. That's the name of our
barracks. It's not much like a fancy hotel but I guess it's
home. We'll probably sleep in much worse places in this
before long.
We have a new papa on the crew. Avery's wife's been
expecting. He called her before we left the states and she
was in the hospital. So he figures by now he's a proud
father, but he's wondering now if it's boy or girl. We all
had cigars on it anyway.
So far I haven't minded my stay overseas but naturally I
haven't been here long enough to know. I suppose I'll have
my fill of it before too long. I can't figure out though, the
war's over in Europe, why didn't they send me there.
Darling, I'm so sleepy I can hardly keep awake while
writing. It's the first chance I've had to write for quite a
while and I did want to write you. After all, it's been three
or four days since I've told you I love you. I do love you
brown eyes so very much. Remember those plans we made,
well sweet we'll have plenty of time from now on for
nothing but planning so let's make some good ones. Then
start praying for the day to come soon when they'll
materialize. Good night sweet, write often, I miss you.
Love forever
Dick

On the morning of May 11th, 1945 Grandpa left Canton for their five hour flight to Tarawa, starting his journey to Nadzab, New Guinea. Then on May 12th, he left Tarawa Island in the morning for his 10-hour flight to Los Negros Island. During their flight, Capone had sighted a submarine and started a search for it, but didn't find it.

They crossed the International Date Line and lost a day. Then he flew 6 hours to Biak, where they left their plane on May 14th. And on May 16th, he left Biak in a C-53 transport plane for a 4-hour flight to finally end up in Nadzab, for assignment to a combat outfit.

CHAPTER 14
Nadzab, New Guinea
Joining the Flying Circus

(Nadzab, New Guinea)

May 20, 1945

My Very Dearest Anna:
How are you this beautiful Sunday morn, honey? Did I say beautiful, my mistake. It's been raining all morning. One good thing though it's much cooler, quite a relief from the heat we've been having.
It takes quite an effort to walk to the mess hall to eat. After about 10 steps the mud is caked so thick on your shoes you can hardly lift them. It's a great life.
I'd feel much better if I would only get a letter from you. I haven't had any mail since I left the states. I figure it should be catching up to me soon though. I've read and

175

reread the last few letters I got at Mather till I know them by heart.

You remember how at Langley I would gripe about the K.P. I found out now that they were looking at the future and giving me needed training for I had K.P. yesterday. It wasn't too bad though, I've had much harder K.P. I also hit a good day for they had creamed turkey for dinner. I guess that's quite a treat over here. It looks to me as though K.P. is an unescapable evil.

I guess I'd better close now, sweet there's not a whole lot to write about. I need mail for inspiration.

I couldn't close without telling you how much I love you. I do love you Anna, you know that. And I miss you so very much. I've never known anyone nearly as sweet as you. You're wonderful brown eyes. I can't wait for this war to end and we're together again. Good night my darling and -

Love forever,
Dick

May 23, 1945

My Very Dearest Anna:

I have a little time for writing so I might as well use it. I haven't had very much of it lately. I'm just getting around to answering the last of your letters I got the other day. I haven't had any since that but I'm hoping.

That class play must have been some show. I can just imagine what it was like. School plays usually aren't very good.

I just got paid a while ago. We use Australian money. I got 10 pounds. It's a pain in the neck using foreign money. It's hard to tell whether you got gypped or not. In the Dutch East Indies it was Dutch money. Guineas and guilders, now it's pounds, shillings, and pence. A pound is worth $3.20 in American just think of what a ton would be worth. (I know that was corny, so what).

By the way, where did you get all the ambition to do all that work of cleaning up the back yard. I haven't had that much ambition and energy as far back as I can remember.

I went out to the pistol range to try out my .45. The gun's no good, it won't hit a doggoned thing. No fooling I need plenty of practice with that gun. I couldn't hit the side of a barn from the inside with it.

Well, sweet, I guess I'll have to sign off for now. Just remember, darling, I love you very much and I always will. You're so wonderful brown eyes, I can't help but love you. So long for now, sweetheart.

Love forever,
Dick

May 24, 1945

My Very Dearest Anna:

I really hit the jackpot today. I have letters galore, 15 of them. The best part of it is that 8 of them were from you. They ranged all the way from Apr. 30 to May 11. I guess now all my mail has caught up. I hope it comes in steady from now on instead of bunches. That way it spreads my morale out over more time. I spent a very enjoyable afternoon reading them all. Now I'm writing by candle light to answer them. I doubt if I can possibly answer all of them tonight. If the candle would hold out I think I would write all night.

You remember me telling you about Avery's wife being in the hospital to have a baby the day we left the states. It's been two weeks now and he still don't know what he's a father of. Steppe just come in with a telegram for him and

177

he's not here. I think we're as anxious as he to find out what it is. After all we smoked the cigars and still don't know what we smoked them for. We'd open the telegram only I know he'd want to be the first to know. He'll probably be back before I'm finished and you can know too. I'll bet five dollars it's a boy. If it is he'll be the only man on the crew. Every other married man on the crew has a girl. Not a single one has a boy.

Spencer is over here now griping. His girl give him the devil because she didn't hear from him for a few days. He's mad now and is going to give her the devil for giving him the devil (still follow me). I'm glad we don't have trouble like that. I'm also very lucky to have such an understanding girlfriend as you. If you weren't so forgiving you'd be mad at me all the time the way the mail comes in.

Naturally, I'll be one of the last on the crew to be promoted. I should get another stripe soon, I keep telling myself. I'd like at least to catch up with Gib and Gene. The pay jump is from $66 to $78 for sergeant. Of course with flight pay and overseas pay it amounts to about a $20 increase. If and when I get the stripe I think I'll increase that allotment to about $60. I'm all for building up my bank account. I found out already that you don't spend much money overseas.

When you mentioned having your picture taken in your formal I immediately tore open the rest of the mail to see if it was in there. Of course I was hoping for a little too much to get it so soon, but I am anxious to see how you look in it. Naturally, you'll look very sweet – you always do. I can picture it in my mind and it makes a very pretty picture. I wish I could be there to see you wear it in person. How very much I wish that. I miss you sweetheart – more than you can tell.

I know how excited you are about graduating. I was too, I was in a stupor trying to believe I was actually through with school. You know me though, I never went out to social functions much. I did go to the prom and banquet though, but I never took a girl. We should have graduated together then I could have taken you. Id' have been the proudest senior to ever graduate from NPHS. Now that you're a woman of the world, darling, I want to wish you the best of luck always. If I were only home now we could start out on those plans of ours.

With you behind me sweet, I'm positive I could make good at anything I tried. The thing I want to do now is get back to the states as soon as I can. I intend making good on that score.

Sweetheart, this candle is burning pretty low. I think that means I'll have to close until tomorrow. I won't seal the letter till I find out about Avery's baby. I'll start writing again first thing in the morning. After all I've only answered one letter so far.

Anna darling – I love you so much. The longer we're apart and the farther away I am from you the more I love you. I can't wait to hold you again and tell you how much I love you personally. Goodnight brown eyes.

Love forever,
Dick

P.S. It's a boy – Johnny

Grandma in her formal dress that she wore to her school dance in 1945.

My Very Dearest Anna:

Here I am up bright and early to do some more writing. After my candle burned down I had to hit the sack. It's much better writing by the bright sunshine though the only trouble is that you can't find the sunshine this morning. The rains came when I was about halfway to the mess hall, and me without a raincoat.

Here it is May and you're still talking about fixing fires. What kind of weather are you having back in Ohio? That

180

*furnace was quite a bother wasn't it? We'd just get settled
so comfortably on the couch and that darned furnace would
come between us. That's the advantage of a fire place. We
could sit in front of it and toss a log on every once in a
while without even getting up.*

*So you don't consider me a pest. Well maybe after
we've been married fifty years you'll realize how much a
pest I am.*

*So you're changing your mind about Washington now, I
imagine jobs are going to be harder to get now that
Germany folded up.*

*I found out quite some time ago that Phila is quite a
small town. But I wouldn't trade it for all the big cities I've
been in. I'll admit being away from home is good
experience but I figure by now I've had enough traveling to
last a lifetime.*

*I can just picture Miss Beaber trying to quiet down that
double study hall. I remember the hard times she had with
ours. We'd almost drive her batty, twanging hair pins,
banging desk tops, sailing paper airplanes across the room.
A teacher really leads a rough life.*

*I think I'll talk Steppe into going after his beer, I'm
pretty thirsty right now. Steppe, Spence, and I have a
system. We're allowed three bottles of beer every three
days. So the first day, I get my three bottles and we each
have a cold bottle of beer. The second day, Steppe gets his
and the third Spence gets his. That way we have a bottle a
day. If we'd all buy it at once we'd either have to drink all
three then or let it set and get warm. We have mental
geniuses on this crew, we have an angle for everything.*

*This is the last sheet of stationery so I'll have to quit till
I beg, borrow or steal some more.*

*Remember sweet, that I love you and I'm thinking of
you every minute. There couldn't be anyone else but you*

for me. *I love you brown eyes and I miss you so much. So long.*

Love always,
Dick

May 26, 1945

My Very Dearest Anna:
   I bought this bracelet off of some guy here who makes them in his spare time. I hope you like it. It's made of English or rather Australian (same difference) coins ground down on one side and engraved the way you want. There's always someone around peddling trinkets but these bracelets are the nicest I've seen over here.
   I hoped I'd hear from you last night and I did. I had one letter from you. I'll answer it this afternoon when I have more time.
   So till then, darling, I love you. And I miss you terribly. I'll be thinking of you brown eyes.

Love always
Dick

My Very Dearest Anna:
  Here I am again, I didn't have quite as much time to write today as I expected but I did want to drop a line.
  There's not much news around here though. I went to the show last night. It was Olsen and Johnson in "See My Lawyer". It was nothing to brag about but it's something to do with an evening. It will be strange to go to an indoor theater again. It's all outdoor shows over here. You just stretch out on the hillside and watch the picture. Naturally, I'd much, very much, rather be sitting in the Quaker with you beside me. That's the only way I can enjoy a movie even if I'm not watching the screen.
  I didn't do much shouting either on V-E Day. I celebrated in Hawaii with free beer. I'm going to do my celebrating when Japan goes down for the count.
  You say your cousin has been engaged for three years. That's an awfully long time isn't it? I certainly don't want for us to be engaged that long before getting married. But then we aren't even engaged yet. But what can I do about it way over here. When I get back to the states though, something will be done about it. Capone seems to think that won't be too long and I hope not but I believe he's inclined to be a little over-optimistic. I guess the important thing is to get back and I've got so much to come back too. I have no doubts about getting back.
  So you have a hard time trying to understand me. I know it's difficult but sometimes I make sense. Just so you understand that I love you very, very much.
  I don't remember how many invitations I sent out but it wasn't many. Why feel as if it's asking for a gift, some people might feel insulted if they didn't get one. It's just a custom, after all, you only graduate once.

*I was only kidding about flirting with the teacher. I'll
admit it would be pretty difficult to flirt with <u>Miss</u> Collins.
I'll have to close for now sweet. How did I ever manage
to fall so much in love with you. I guess it's because you're
so sweet and so lovable. There's no one on earth I'd rather
love, there' no one nearly as wonderful as you. I love you
brown eyes and I miss you terribly. So long darling. I'll be
thinking of you.*

Always
Dick

May 29, 1945

My Very Dearest Anna:
    *Yesterday was my day for mail again. It comes in
bunches every 2 or 3 days. I had three wonderful letters
from you so I'm in a good mood again.*
    *We're having a little more rain this morning, not much
but it's keeping it cool at least. There's quite a breeze
flowing through the tent. I'll have to find something to
weight these letters down or they'll be blowing all over
camp.*
    *Didn't you like "A Tree Grows in Brooklyn"? It was
rather sad in spots but I thought it was fairly good for that
type of show.*
    *Mom was telling me how they fixed up the house. Those
two sure put up a lot of effort keeping up that house. I hope
I have as much ambition on our own and I think I will, but I
doubt if I could be as handy as Dad. That guy's never
happy unless he's puttering around with something. I hope
that old saying "like father, like son" is true. It would be
more fun fixing up your own house. Then you have more
pride in it. No I don't think white wood work would be
practical unless you would want to be washing it all the*

time. There's not only little kids to worry about. I know Mom was always after me for marking up the woodwork on the kitchen door frame.

I'm sorry you didn't enjoy yourself at the class dance. I know what you mean by that certain set that think they are all it. We had them in our class and I guess they're in every class.

Personally, I just ignore them. If they only knew they're not as uppity as they think.

I can't write much more right now, sweet, I have a few things to do at the moment but I'll try to write again after a while.

Don't forget though darling, I love you with all my heart. You're tops brown eyes there's no one as wonderful as you – that's why I love you so dog-goned much. I miss you sweet.

Love Forever,
Dick

On the morning of May 30th, 1945, Grandpa left Nadzab heading to Biak at noon for refueling. He eventually landed in Morotai, where he spent the night in a transient camp. On May 31st, he took off in the morning and landed at Zamboanga Field on Mindinao for refueling. He then proceeded to the Island of Mindoro in the Philippines, where he was assigned to the 380th Bomber Group, 530th Bomber Squadron as part of the 5th Air Corps.

In June, Grandma moved to Washington D.C. with a friend, to work at the Pentagon.

CHAPTER 15
Mindoro, Philippines
Bombing Missions

Grandpa flew his first mission on June 4th, 1945, with their target in Borneo. These are the first two sets of Grandpa's notes from his missions.

MONDAY – JUNE 4, 1945
FIRST MISSION

Four days after joining 530th, we flew our first mission. We were awakened at 3:30 A.M., ate a hearty (?) breakfast of pancakes and coffee, briefed at 0400. Target was industrial town of Miri in Borneo, never before hit by 380th. Little known what sort of reception we'd get.

It began raining as we started engines. I was pretty well drenched by take-off time. We started take-off and plane swerved on the slippery runway so we taxied around and tried again. Take-off time was 0620. Co-pilot was Wilkinson, two gunners, Jarvis and Mason were finishing missions on this one.

Our ship was No. 209 "Rough Knight" with close to 100 missions racked up on it. Weather was rough that day and we flew extended formation to target.

We made run on target after joining formation. Capone pulled out of run just as bombs went away, dropping them in ocean. Other planes made good hits on target. No flak fired at us at all. One ship claimed lone fighter attacked them shooting tracers past tail. No one saw the plane though and credit for interception was refused. It was positive "milk run". We even circled target couple times to allow photographers to get good pictures. We run into more rough weather on way back. Landing time was 1620.

FLIGHT TIME – 10 Hrs. 00 min.
TOTAL TIME – 10 Hrs. 00 min.

POINTS SCORED – 2 pts.
TOTAL POINTS – 2 pts.

FRIDAY – JUNE 15, 1945
SECOND MISSION

After unusual delay of 11 days credited to bad weather, we flew our second mission. Kaufman was bombardier, Reed was grounded for small operation on back. Price, new crew member, Noonan, and Daley flew first mission this time.

Target was to be industrial town 2/3 up coast of Formosa, named Taichu. Take off time was 0625. We lost formation from beginning and flew lone wolf entire mission.

Around 11:30 we spotted other planes returning from target so we decided not to bomb original target but pick out something near by. We tried Mako Naval Base, bombs away at 11:44 but no hits scored.

We spotted a few flak bursts on bomb run but they missed our number and we weren't holed. I saw about four bursts 9 o'clock level, were fairly close but not enough to do damage.

There were no fighters sent against us. We landed at 1647.

Our ship was again 209 "Rough Knight". Perfect weather all the way. The "Knight" cracked up next morning on take-off, but no one was hurt and only minor damage done to plane.

FLIGHT TIME – 10 Hrs. 22 min.
TOTAL TIME – 20 Hrs. 22 min.

POINTS SCORED – 2+ pts.
TOTAL POINTS – 4+ pts.

Nose art for Rough Night, Grandpa's plane during his first and second mission.

On June 18th, 1945, Japenese resistance ended in Mindanao in the Phillipines. Meanwhile in the United States, President Truman approved the invasion of mainland Japan.

Cpl. R.B. Moore
A.S.N. 35922674
A.P.O. 19194-BW-8
c/o Postmaster

San Francisco, Calif.
(Mindoro)

Miss Anna Wyatt
208 St. Clair Ave. S.W.
New Philadelphia
Ohio

June 18, 1945

My Very Dearest Anna:

Here I am again as I said but I may not be able to stay long. I was wondering about writing to your Phila address but I'll keep writing anyway till I get the new one. I suppose your Mom will forward your mail.

I don't mind reading a lot of letters at one time, by the time I get it I'm glad there's so much to read. Naturally, I'd prefer it to be spread out and get some every day, but then who wouldn't?

I'll never regard your letters in the same light as Gene did Ethel's. After all, I don't think he cares nearly as much for her as I do for you. That makes quite a difference. Your letters are far from the "same old stuff", each one seems better than the last. I'll never die from boredom reading a letter from you that's sure.

You are getting to be in the money now. That was a swell present from your Dad. You know I used to be half afraid of your Dad before I got to know him. But especially after that last furlough I'm convinced he's a swell guy.

Honey, I'm going to marry you for your money yet. You have good job now you can support the family while I take a nice long vacation. I know you're not taking me serious, I hope. About the money part I mean.

I figured I'd have to cut this short when I started. It's about time for the lights to go out. In fact they just went

out, I'm finishing by flashlight. Tomorrow's another day
and I can write again then. So till tomorrow brown eyes,
good night. I love you and miss you very much.

Love forever,
Dick

Japanese resistance ends on Okinawa as the US Tenth Army completes its capture on June 22nd, 1945. The Battle of Okinawa was one of the bloodiest battles of WWII. Nearly three months later, Grandpa would arrive on Okinawa to stay for a duration of four months.

Cpl. R.B. Moore
A.S.N. 35922674
530th Bomb Sqdn., 380th Bomb Gp.
A.P.O. 321 c/o Postmaster
San Francisco, California, U.S.A.

Miss Anna Wyatt
208 St. Clair Ave. S.W.
New Philadelphia
Ohio

June 23, 1945

My Very Dearest Anna:
    Today's my lucky day for I heard from you again. It
was dated May 30 so you hadn't left for Washington yet. I
also had a letter from Mom direct to my new A.P.O. so now
that it's coming here I should get mail more regularly.
    I slept till dinnertime today. I was on guard duty all last
night. We didn't get to drive in a jeep this time so it was a

mighty tiresome six hours. I believe I was asleep even before I got into bed.

As usual, it is raining. You know after so long you gradually get accustomed to this weather. I haven't seen the sun for so long I forget what it looks like. I wish it would come out if only for a couple seconds just to break the monotony of things. I believe it has actually rained more this last week than it did on my furlough. Remember every time we'd go somewhere together, it would rain.

I know what you mean about a shopping tour being work. When Mom was visiting at Langley Field, she went shopping. We walked the streets of Newport News and visited every store in the town or so it seemed. By the time I got back to the field, I was ready to hit the sack. Once a woman goes shopping there's no stopping her till she has seen every dress, hat and pair of shoes in town. And it always ends up the same way, after all that shopping they end up buying a couple handkerchiefs.

I know that they say the native women get whiter every time you look at them honey, but evidently I haven't been overseas long enough for my eyesight to be impaired for they still look the same shade.

I certainly hope they have a good show tonight. I haven't seen one for over a week. Last night they had Laurel and Hardy again. It was here a couple weeks ago and they brought it back. I'm sure it wasn't by popular demand.

This new writing table we built is all right. It's right in the corner of the tent with a nice cool breeze blowing through. You look out and you have a wonderful view of the scenic Philippine Island. That's what I call writing in perfect comfort. All I need is a cold mint julep to make the setting perfect.

I'm awfully anxious to get your new Washington address and hear how you're getting along back there.

192

Mom said Dort heard from you and you liked it there. I'll bet you get a little touch of homesickness though.

Well, darling, I'll sign off for this time. Just remember brown eyes that I love you and I miss you more than words can tell. You're wonderful Anna, that's why I love you so dog-goned much. So long for now.

Love always,

Dick

SUNDAY – JUNE 24, 1945
THIRD MISSION

Our pilot was Lutsey; Capone grounded with cold. Target was Balikpapan in Borneo, "Ploesti of South Pacific". Take-off time 0620.

Our first really good mission. We kept formation and made good hits on target. Our bomb load was nine 500 pounders. Our target was Ack-Ack positions around Balikpapan area. Made good hits, unknown as to whether positions were knocked out.

About a half-hour from target we caught slight amount of ack-ack, none fired while over target. We had small, very small, hole below waist window. Was slight dispute as to whether it was flak hole but anohter ship in formation was holed and settled all disputes.

No fighter interception was even anticipated. We only carried light load of ammo, only about 100 rds. per gun.

After completion of bomb run, I spotted another group, probably 90th B.G. several thousand feet below, hitting coastline close to target, also much of the adjoining water.

We ran into very little bad weather. Landing time was 1925. Our ship this time was No. 370, "Mary M."

193

FLIGHT TIME – 13 Hrs. 05 min.
TOTAL TIME – 33 Hrs. 27 min.

POINTS SCORED – 2 ½+ (possible 3 ½)
TOTAL POINTS – 7 ½+

Nose art of "Mary M".

The Borneo Campaign began on May 1st, 1945 continuing through July 21st. It was the last major Allied campaign in the South Pacific during World War II. In a series of amphibious assaults, the Australian I Corps attacked Japanese forces occupying the island.

The last amphibious assault of World War II was the Battle of Balikpapan starting on July 1st, 1945. Prior to the amphibious landing, Balikpapan had been hit by heavy bombing from Australian and U.S. air and naval forces, which Grandpa took part in for his third and fourth missions. Major operations had come to an end by July 21, 1945.

(Mindoro)

June 26, 1945

My Very Dearest Anna:
Here I am back again. I'm mess hall guard tonight. That's in case someone gets so hungry they want to break into the mess hall for something to eat. So I have all night to six in the morning to write. I should get all my mail answered at that rate.

As I told you in my letter this morning I received my first letter from you direct to the squadron. There's still a lapse from May 26 to June 13 that probably went through New Guinea and will catch up later.

I've been wondering if you ever got that bracelet I sent you from Guinea. You may have mentioned it in one of the letters I haven't received yet. I was doubtful if it would go through but they assured me it would and I sent it. The rest of the guys sent them too and haven't heard.

I understand perfectly how it is not having enough time to write. I remember the resolution I made to write you every day. I doubted when I made it if I'd be able to keep it but I was at least going to try. I believe I'll quit making resolutions for I never have been able to keep them. I hope you're able to write that long letter telling all about

Washington and your work. I didn't see much of the town when I was on my way home, but it looked pretty nice.

From the way you talk it must be pretty warm back there. What kind of room do you have? From what they say about housing conditions in the Capitol I'd guess that you wouldn't have any place extraordinary.

You should know by now how you rate with me, sweet. Do you think I've been joking all this time. I may do a lot of kidding, but I'm very serious about you. I've been planning on getting engaged when I get back to the states. How long that will be I don't know. I figure on it being a year at least. We can figure out the wedding date after that, undoubtedly soon after that. I love you Anna, no two ways about it.

We've known one another quite a while, it's been at least six years, hasn't it. Sometimes I've been so mad at you I didn't care if I ever seen you again. But my anger never held out long.

I used to be plenty jealous of Henry. Remember the night we went to the midnight show you and Henry, Flo and Gene, Nug and I. I didn't enjoy that show at all, not as you thought I did. All the time I was wishing I were with you instead. It's a heck of a note when you have to compete with your own cousin for the girl you love. Mom always used to kid me about who was going to win out, Henry or I. I guess that questions settled now.

I'll tell what I did in Hawaii when Walt Noonan met his brother. It was quite an event so we all decided to celebrate. We all had a couple quarts we brought over to sell or use personally. That night we decided against selling it and for using it. I was slightly inebriated before the night was over. Steppe told me that I sat on his bed and talked to him for over an hour about getting our missions in so I could get back to the states and marry Anna. He said I even invited him to be best man.

196

I know your opinion on drinking and after that night I wholeheartedly agree with you so don't think I've made it a habit.

That's not the only time I ever talked about getting married either. Steppe and Noonan are both married and their wives and babies are their favorite subjects so I've heard quite a bit on married life from them. This war can't last too much longer, maybe it won't be too far in the future before we can start on our plans.

I dreamt about you in Washington last night. I was hitchhiking into the city. The guy I was riding with left me out in front of a big office building. There were a bunch of girls going back to work from lunch. I spotted you looking in a store window and started running to you. You saw me and started running to me. Just then I stopped dreaming but I imagine it was quite a collision. I doubt if you'll ever see me coming down the street in Washington but it was a swell dream anyway.

I guess I'd better give your eyes a rest for now darling so I'll sign off for now. I miss you so much brown eyes, more than you know. Good night sweet, I love you.

Love forever,
Dick

<u>THURSDAY – JUNE 28, 1945</u>
<u>FOURTH MISSION</u>

For the first time we had our complete crew flying together. Target was Sepinggan airdrome, few miles from Balikpapan. Take-off time was 0630.

Our bomb load was 38 - 100 pounders. Missed out on formation again and expected to have to hit target alone again. Fortunately we beat formation to target, spotted them and joined them for bomb run. The target was obscured by clouds so an H2X* run was made, toggling off lead ship. We couldn't see where bombs hit.

Immediately after bombs away the flak began to come up. I spotted first burst at 6 o'clock fairly close. Our ship was unscathed but one ship in formation was holed. We had light load of ammo as on previous mission and no fighters were sighted.

We hit roughest weather yet on return to base. Landing time was 1945.

Our ship was No. 323 "Lucky Star".

FLIGHT TIME – 13 Hrs. 15 min.
TOTAL TIME – 46 Hrs. 42 min.

POINTS SCORED – 2 ½+ (possible 3 ½)
TOTAL POINTS – 11 ½+

*H2X radar was a navigation system used for overcast and nighttime bomb runs.

(Mindoro)

My Very Dearest Anna:

We had our fireworks display tonight. The officers were up on the hill shooting off parachute flares. I'll admit it wasn't quite as spectacular as the Tuscora Park display, but it was better than nothing. The Fourth used to be something to look forward to. Stock up for weeks ahead on all types of firecrackers and then proceed to drive the more quiet citizens crazy with the noise for a few days. Then when the din was over, parents and neighbors settle back with a sigh of relief for another year.

Remember a couple years ago we were at the park, ditched everyone else, watched the fireworks and walked home. Of course your Dad didn't know where you got to. When I come home Mom said he was looking for you and would probably tear me in half. I doubt if he'd do anything quite so drastic. I think his confidence in me has increased since that time.

We moved into our new tent this afternoon. There's still quite a bit of work to be done. We have it wallpapered with our Langley Field pin-ups plus a few not quite so modest we picked up in Kansas City. That bamboo is a hard substance to put thumbtacks in, so I found out by wearing callouses on my thumb. Those pin-ups at Langley were a study in psychology. Every time the inspecting officer walked in our room, his eyes would bulge and light up with satisfaction, he'd mutter "Fine taste, men", he'd never look at the room to see if it was clean. Needless to say we passed every inspection. In fact before we left the same officer visited us and wheedled a few of our finest selections from us. He's probably admiring them in his barracks at Langley right at this moment.

I should be quite clean tonight. I went down to take a shower, it's at the bottom of the hill which is slick as ice

199

with nice slimy mud. So I showered felt quite healthy and satisfied and started the journey back to the tent. Halfway up the hill my feet neatly slid from under me and I was very much in need of another shower. They say when you become a civilian again you look back on your Army days and get a big kick out of your experiences. So if someday in the future you see me suddenly curl up on the floor and die laughing you'll know the cause of it.

I haven't heard from you in three days now, so I'm behind on the news of happenings in the metropolis of Washington. I'd like to know how you like your new job.

I hope you don't decide to make a career of secretarial work for I have a different type of career outlined for you. Would you rather be slaving over a hot stove or a hot typewriter?

It seems that someone sneaked up on me and tied 50 lb. weights to my eyelids. At least it feels that way for I'm gradually going to sleep, my favorite state of mind. So I'd better sign off for now, and try out this new sack. It's not on the down hill trend it was in the other tent so maybe I can sleep a little better. I think I'm due for a much deserved rest after working so hard on our new quarters (who am I trying to kid, you or myself?).

So good night for now, darling, as always I love you very much. You're wonderful, brown eyes. I miss you.

Love always,

Dick

July 6, 1945

My Very Dearest Anna:

Today was another of those lucky days I look forward to. Four wonderful letters from you, what more could I ask for? (Four more letters.)

The one letter was the one written on the train I guessed that at the first glance, it was pretty shaky. It don't make much difference whether you travel day or night by train. It's always monotonous.

We went swimming at the beach this afternoon. Not exactly swimming, riding the surf. Those waves come tearing in way over your head. The boys got quite a kick out of me. I ventured out to try my luck. You know I'm no swimmer. The first big wave caught me and took me head over heels back to shore. Noonan was standing there laughing when another caught him off guard and he followed me right in. It was a lot of fun. We've planned on going down the past two weeks but never could get enough ambition.

Would you really like to go to Washington for a vacation? I think it would be better to go somewhere you haven't been. After I get to be a big executive and able to dictate my own working hours we'll take quite a few vacations, travel all over the states. Of course, we'll have a big Packard, gas and tires will be plentiful and we can travel to our own hearts' content. Big talk for a little guy, isn't it.

You're lucky to work in an air-conditioned office. After a day like this I wouldn't mind doing a little bit of complaining about the cold. For once it didn't rain, but it was plenty hot.

I didn't think Joe and Adeline would make a go of their marriage. I'm surprised it lasted that long. I don't think any of the Mowls had a successful marriage. They're always beating their wives and breaking furniture. They used to live across from Ma and the police were there all the time. That was the old St. Clair St. always something going on. It had quite a reputation in those days. The police used to patrol it regularly. It's a wonder they didn't move

201

the station down there. It's tamed down quite a bit now though.

That's quite a cartoon my sister sent you. That character on the left does resemble me quite a bit, but the other doesn't look at all like you. We never had much trouble with the neighbors though, except for Alexanders. I always wanted to throw a stone at that porch light of theirs.

I must have swallowed some of the salt water at the beach today for I've been thirsty ever since we got back. I could stand a good cold coke right now. I think I'd even settle for a big pitcher of cold draught beer like we had at Mather Field. I'd better stop thinking of those things my tongue is hanging out now. Spence and I were just going to make some coffee but the stove is giving us a little trouble and we had to give up the idea. So I guess I'll have to resort to plain water, maybe with a strong imagination it might taste like beer. Nope, I'm afraid my power of imagination isn't quite up to the task. It still taste like plain water.

Well, sweet, I guess it comes time to sign off for now. As always, brown eyes, remember I love you very much. And I miss you more than you know.

Love forever,
Dick

SATURDAY – JULY 7, 1945
FIFTH MISSION

Pilot was Rush; Capone grounded for breach of radio discipline. Bombardier was Shilling, Reed in hospital with yellow jaundice. Reed had narrow escape week before flying with other crew, has been pretty nervous since. Target was Matsuyama on Northern tip of Formosa. We

202

were after several planes on the ground at airdrome. Take-off time 0630.

Bomb load was 158 small frags. We stayed with formation all the way, perfect weather out and back. Target was slightly obscured by clouds. Bombs did damage to runways but missed planes.

Hell broke loose on bomb run. Ample flak, and I mean ample. They had our number right from the start but there were no hits. One ship was holed three times. I saw one white phosphorus shell burst close to formation. Pilot claims he saw a small box-like affair tumbling past plane, emitting small, square "stuff", he describes it. Probably a new type of anti-aircraft shell.

This mission was our first for interception. Two planes made a pass at our formation. There were defugalties as to types of planes. Our boy said silver, radial-engine jobs. It was high, frontal attack, only nose and upper got to fire. I saw them pass overhead but couldn't recognize them.

We had good weather again.

Our ship was 323 "Lucky Star".

Landing time – 1905.

FLIGHT TIME – 12 Hrs. 35 min.
TOTAL TIME – 59 Hrs. 17 min.

POINTS SCORED – 2 ½+ (probable 6 ½)
1 pt. A.A. and 1 pt. Interc.
TOTAL POINTS – 16+

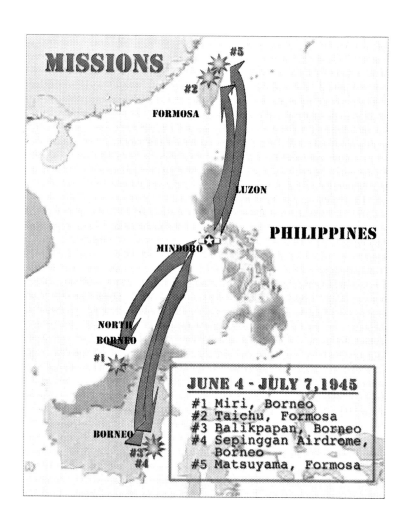

MISSIONS

#5

#2

FORMOSA

LUZON

PHILIPPINES

MINDORO

NORTH
BORNEO

#1

BORNEO

#3
#4

JUNE 4 - JULY 7, 1945
#1 Miri, Borneo
#2 Taichu, Formosa
#3 Balikpapan, Borneo
#4 Sepinggan Airdrome,
   Borneo
#5 Matsuyama, Formosa

Sgt. Richard B. Moore
A.S.N. 35922674
530th Bomb Sqdn., 380th Bomb Gp.
A.P.O. 321 c/o Postmaster
San Francisco, California, U.S.A.
 (Mindoro)

204

July 11, 1945

My Very Dearest Anna:
  I doubt if I'll get much writing done tonight it's pretty late but I wanted to get off a few lines anyway.
  I didn't hear from you today. I finally heard from Gene though. He sent a picture of a French girl he went with – not bad either. I'm inclined to think that cousin of mine is a first class wolf. His mail is no longer censored, he told me a little of the work he'd be doing. He's sweating out now whether or not they send him back to the states or send him this way. He said if he gets to come home it won't be till November anyway.
  I think Carol sounds like a nice name. But don't promise too many people to name children after them. We'd have quite a family in order to keep the promises.
  I don't have any trouble getting stamps, darling. Thanks anyway for thinking of it. I've been using the stamped envelopes but I still have a couple books of stamps I brought from the states.
  After your story of crowded conditions in the place you live at Washington I'd say our little tent was a cozy, comfortable affair.
  Our friend the chicken paid us another visit this morning and again left us its token of appreciation for a good roosting place. I lost in the drawing for the egg again but if it don't get discouraged and disinherit us I'm bound to win within the next four days.

It started raining again a while ago and I sprung a new leak above my sack. It's not big enough to bother with now, I hope. If I'm wrong I'll know about it before morning.

We're having visitors in the form of rats around here now. One got in Steppe's bag and made a feast of one of his sheets.

He had it folded neatly and now when he opens it out he has a pretty design of about eight holes in the sheet. We found a cat and got in its good graces so if it stays with us we should be rid of the rodents in short order. What with rats, cats, and chickens this tent is becoming slightly overcrowded. Next thing you know we'll have a menagerie in here and we'll be sleeping in the rain, forced out by the animal kingdom.

I'll have to close now, brown eyes. Have I ever said I love you. I guess I did but I'll say it again – I love you, Anna and miss you terribly. Good night sweet and –

Love Always,

Dick

CHAPTER 16
The Atomic Bomb

On July 17th, 1945, Grandpa took off in a B-24 around noon from Mindoro and landed at Floridablanca on Luzon to tear down the "Flying Circus" camp. Then on July 29th, he and his crew loaded onto trucks for a three hour trip through Zig-Zag Pass to Subic Bay, where he would load a LST (Landing Ship, Tank).

Late in the evening of August 5th, Grandpa was scheduled for an early morning bombing mission the next day. During the mission briefing, they were told that it was possible that they might not make it back. They were told that no more than 500 anti-aircraft guns could be pointed at you at one time. The following morning, they found a post on the board that their mission had been canceled.

Aircraft from the 5th and 7th Air Corps were on bombing missions over the mainland of Japan on August 5th, so I would assume that Grandpa and his crew were going to bomb the mainland for their mission the following day.

On August 6th, 1945, the B-29 superfortress named *Enola Gay* dropped the first atomic bomb on Hiroshima. So when Grandpa showed up in the morning for his flight, there was a notice that all missions were cancelled due to the dropping of the atomic bomb. Whenever he would tell this story, he would grab my hand silently and his eyes would tear up. Never saying it, but you knew what he believed. That he wouldn't be coming home if they had flown that mission, this huge moment in history perhaps had saved his life.

The B-29 Superfortress, Enola Gay.

So instead of flying a mission on August 6th, Grandpa loaded and embarked on LST No. 799 for a trip to Okinawa. During the trip there were several air raid scares but no actual attacks.

The second atomic bomb was dropped on Nagasaki three days later on August, 9th. This attack persuaded Japan to pursue peace immediately and lead to the end of the war.

On August 11th, the LST that Grandpa was on board dropped anchor in a harbor off of Okinawa. He had heard news of pending peace the night before. Four days later on August 15th, VJ Day is declared, ending the war with Japan.

CHAPTER 17
Okinawa

Sgt. Richard B. Moore
A.S.N. 35922674
530th Bomb Sqdn., 380th Bomb Gp.
A.P.O. 337 c/o P.M.
San Francisco, Calif.
(Okinawa)

> *Miss Anna Wyatt*
> *208 St. Clair Ave. S.W.*
> *New Philadelphia*
> *Ohio*

August 28, 1945

My Very Dearest Anna:

I seem to be having quite a busy time of it. I had K.P. yesterday, detail this afternoon and guard duty tonight. I don't know, we've had three new duty sergeants this week yet my name seems to stick with each one and every time there's work, I get it. Oh well, seeing as how I got out of the habit of work in the Army I'd better acquire the habit again or I won't do any work in civilian life. And how are we going to support a family without money.

But all this work does affect my time and I don't get much writing done. I haven't been receiving much mail either. There's a hold up somewhere. I had a letter from you dated the 18th and there's a few missing before that.

Yesterday was one of my bad days. I was on K.P. and that's enough to take the brightness out of any day. We finished with breakfast about nine. The Captain sent a guy to tell us our tent had to be taken down by noon, just when I'd settled comfortably in the sack. So down come the tent, then came the alarming fact that supply had no new tents. There we were, no tent over our beds and baggage, no tent to be had, blood pressure rapidly rising when the mess officer sent for us to go back on K.P. To top it off it began to cloud up. There was three of the crew on K.P. , the other three managed to find a tent and put it up before it rained. I had an outside job on K.P., when it started to rain I kept working to finish up and get back to the tent and got drenched completely in the process.

Our old tent had been condemned because of a rip that leaked when it rained. So imagine my disgust when I walked in the new (?) tent, soaked to the skin and discovered the tent leaked like a sieve, not just in one small spot that bothered nobody, but it leaked all over, drenching everybody. They say when you're out of the Army you'll look back on such events and laugh, but all I can say "Tain't funny, McGee, tain't funny".

That cartoon you sent was pretty sharp. I could use company back in the tail but it would be sort of crowded with both of us in the turret. That might not be so bad either.

So you enjoyed watching the planes take off over the boat on your ride to Mt. Vernon. It wouldn't be so pleasant if you had them taking off right overhead all the time as we do here. The airstrip is headed right over our camp area and every morning, better than any alarm clock, they wake me up in time for breakfast. Just in case one of them don't get altitude soon enough we keep the tent flaps raised so it will go right through without knocking down the tent.

I'll have to get ready for guard duty now darling, one good thing I'll be off tomorrow afternoon and I can get some of my writing done. So till tomorrow brown eyes, I'll sign off. Remember sweet, I love you very much. It would be swell if I would get home this year but don't count on it, it's not probable. Good night, darling, I miss you.

Love forever,
Dick

Sgt. Richard B. Moore
A.S.N. 35922674
530th Bomb Sqdn., 380th Bomb Gp.
A.P.O. 337 c/o P.M.
San Francisco, Calif.
(Okinawa, Ryukyu Islands)

Miss Anna Wyatt
208 St. Clair Ave. S.W.
New Philadelphia
Ohio

Sept. 2, 1945

My Very Dearest Anna:

At last we have a day off. Now maybe I can catch up on some of the writing I'm so far behind in. I have a regular job now. Instead of pulling guard duty and details I'm working on the line. Steppe and I are electricians now. It's no easier than details. But I like it much better.

There seems to be a slow down in mail lately. It's been quite a while since I last heard from you. Maybe today's my lucky day, I hope.

It looks like we're in for a storm. If it rains along with this wind that's blowing I'm liable to get a little wet. We haven't had any rain for a few days so the mud is pretty well dried up.

I can just picture the G.I.'s in Washington celebrating. I'm afraid I didn't get plastered. In fact it's been quite a while since I've had anything to drink, except for beer. I didn't do any celebrating as far as that goes. To me, the war isn't over till we're together again. Till then, I can see no reason for celebration.

The camp's coming along pretty well by now. It shouldn't be too long before it's all set up. It's been a lot of work, maybe once it's complete we'll have more time off.

You have high hopes, hoping for me to be home for Christmas. I guess I have the same the same thing in mind but I doubt it honey, it just don't seem possible. I tell you though, in my opinion, times a wastin'. There's lots of things I have planned and I sure can't do anything about those plans over here.

I finally saw a movie I hadn't seen last night, they had "The Valley of Decision" with Greer Garson. One night here they had an old one of Dick Powell that come out first in 1937. They do ring in a new one every once in a while just to break the monotony.

I just heard that the peace treaty was finally signed and today was declared V-J Day. I guess it's really over, I wondered when they'd sign it. It sure sounds good, it's hard to believe in a way.

It's beginning to look as though I won't get that other stripe. The orders should be through by now if they're going through. I'm satisfied with Sgt. anyway. I never expected to get that far when I first got in the army. I'm still on flying status though, even if I haven't done any flying in quite a while.

We haven't been paid for two months now. That'll make quite a pile of dough when I finally get it. That shows you how much money's needed around here. Two months without pay and I still have five bucks in my pocket. It will seem funny to get back where you're broke a week after payday. But I won't mind it, in fact, I think I could stand a few months being a spend thrift.

They have a project underway here making a book of the activities of the 380th. It will make a nice souvenir to look through in the later years. I imagine it will take quite a while for them to complete it though. Avery's on the business staff. He's a good a good man for the job. He watches his money like a scrooge.

Noonan's in here griping. He gets K.P. on our day off. I think I'd do quite a bit of howling too in a case like that. My turn should be coming around soon, too soon to suit me. Just so there's no more pots and pans to wash in the rain. I won't mind it too much.

Speaking of rain, it's beginning to come down now. I'll have to cover my belongings up or they'll get soaked. I'll close for this time, honey. This is the day we've been looking forward to, but the biggest day is yet to come. Till we're together again brown eyes, remember I love you and I think you're wonderful. So long for now sweet. I miss you and -

Love Forever,
Dick

S. Sgt. Richard B. Moore
A.S.N. 35922674
530th Bomb Sqdn., 380th Bomb Gp.
A.P.O. 337 c/o P.M.
San Francisco, Calif.
(Okinawa)

Miss Anna Wyatt
208 St. Clair Ave. S.W.
New Philadelphia
Ohio

Sept. 4, 1945

My Very Dearest Anna:
    I don't suppose I'll do much writing tonight, it all depends on how long these candles hold out. It won't be long before these nights by candlelight are over, no more cussing every time the wind blows our light out. They have the wires strung for electric lights, they should be on the next day or two.
    I had a surprise this evening. I found out I've been Staff Sgt. since August 1. You have to be a mind reader to know things around here.
    I haven't heard from you for a while. I suppose it's because you were getting ready to go back to Phila. I'll bet things will start to liven up around town again with so many guys coming home. Of course it never was too lively, but there's always plenty going on.

Mom sent me the clipping about Barney Graham. That was certainly a shock. There's quite a few guys I knew and went to school with that were killed.

I saw a good movie last night for a change. "The Big Sleep" with Bogart and Bacall. They're really a good team.

Mom said Gene expected to get home this month. I'll bet Ethel is glad, but maybe Gene isn't as anxious to see her as she is to see him. If he does like her at all he never shows it. Maybe they'll be married by the time I get home. By the way, he said if he beat me home he'd give you a kiss for me, you know, doing me a favor. When he does get home remind him of the fact, for I think that cousin of mine is a little more wolfish than he used to be.

You know it was about a year ago that our crew was formed. Our first anniversary, of course there are only a few of the original crew here. Burns and Bill Angelini are back in the states yet. Pickhardt, our first co-pilot, went to England, flew his missions and is back in the states. There are only four of us left, the rest joined the crew as we went along. We ought to celebrate if we had something to celebrate with. There isn't even any beer around.

Darling, I'm afraid the candle don't have much further to go so I'll have to sign off for tonight. As always, brown eyes, I love you and I miss you very much. Good night sweet, and –

Love forever,
Dick

Grandma didn't stay too long in D.C. Grandpa told me the story about Grandma's stay in Washington. Her landlord was a drunk and she came in screaming at Grandma and her friend that they hadn't paid the rent. But they had paid the rent, they just didn't have a receipt. So they decided that they would be much happier back in New Philadelphia.

Sept. 7, 1945

My Very Dearest Anna:
I'm writing from a novel place tonight. I'm in the show area waiting for the movie to start. We built a bench and set it in the area so we'd always have a reserved seat. Now they announced there'll be no reserved seats, you can leave the benches here but it's first come first served. So in order to keep our seat someone has to be here first. Here I am now holding down the fort. "The Great John L." is on tonight. It sounds good, I'll be able to tell you for sure afterward. I don't imagine I'll finish up before it starts.

I'm in a good mood tonight at least. I had a letter from you. It was from Phila, so I see you're back in the old hometown at last. To even better my good mood the pictures I've been so anxiously waiting for so long were in the letter. And you hoped I wouldn't be disappointed after waiting so long. Darling, I think they're wonderful. So far since I received them at four, I've looked at them for a whole two hours. You said they didn't turn out good but they show you just as sweet as you are and that's plenty good. The longer I look at the pictures the more I wish I were on my way to New Phila. right now.

A B-32 just took off over the area here. They have several up on the line and they're certainly big ships. I was inside. You have all the room of a hotel lobby in one of those giants. They never flew many missions before the war ended. There's another case that increased my dislike and distrust in the Japanese. About a week after the Japs asked for peace and we laid off bombing them, the B-32s went over Japan on a photo mission. 16 Zeroes jumped them and

216

shot hell out of them, killing one gunner and wounding another. Those boys neither expected nor were too well prepared for anything like that. So when our boys went over on a photo mission after that they had a load of bombs and were told to drop them where it would do most good if they were fired on. And if any enemy planes attacked to fire on them in a "friendly" fashion. But they didn't bother us so the boys come back with the bombs.

We flew today. It was just a local flight checking out a pilot. What a ride, I'd sooner fly combat. I was just flying to get my time in.

They're up there cutting engines, banks and turns that shouldn't be made in a 24. Then we made four touch and go landings for practice. The first one he was coming in side ways to the runway. If Steppe hadn't raised the landing gear in time it would have been a rough landing. We were too low and too fast. We were so low if the gear would be down they'd have hit the ground and at the speed we were going the gear wouldn't stay with us long if it would hit. Then to finish the flight the nose wheel tire blew out just as we turned in the revetment to park. If we had made one more landing with that tire we'd have scooted along the runway on our nose. By the way the name of the ship is "Double Trouble", quite appropriate I'd say.

The show's over and I'm back in the tent. It was a pretty good show. At least, they're getting shows over here I haven't seen.

Darling to prevent you from getting gray hairs, which I'm sure wouldn't look good at your age I promise not to go so long without writing again unless it's absolutely unavoidable as it was when I took a boat ride.

Don't worry sweet, when I come home you'll know about it no matter what time night or day. I know on my furloughs when I'd get there at night I didn't want to

217

*awaken you and waited till the next day, but it's certainly
going to be different this time.*

*The latest news on going home is this but it's not
official – There are 33 crews in this squadron. They are
going to send the 15 oldest home – We're number 16 in the
outfit. The peacetime strength will be 18 crews. Figure it
out – we're 18th from the bottom. So no matter how you
figure we're stuck. Although the good part of it is we're
first in line to leave the next time anyone goes. I guess I'd
be expecting too much to go home right away, but I
wouldn't argue about it.*

*George Reed was in after the show, naturally the first
thing I done was show him your pictures. He agrees that I
have a wonderful girlfriend.*

*I couldn't tell you about Reed's close call before but he
did have one, it would happen to him, the most nervous guy
on the crew. He was flying a mission with another crew to
make up for a time he was grounded. That was back on
Mindoro. About the middle of the morning here comes
George in our tent with a half a quart in one hand and he
was shaking. He said "Fellows, can you get me a quart
somewhere, I want to get plastered." We asked what the
trouble was and believe me he had them. They took off and
was out about a half hour when an engine caught fire,
another cut out and still another started throwing oil.
Something must have been wrong with the fourth for it was
functioning perfectly. They started losing altitude and the
pilot ordered to bail out. George stood looking at the
flames shooting past the waist windows and thought "this
is it". They were standing by the hatch to go out deciding
who'd go first when one fellow come running back, pushed
them aside and actually dove out the hatch. George stood
over the hatch ready to go out when he noticed the flames
dying down so he called the pilot and found out everything
was alright. Reed has been in two crashes and bailed out*

once back in the states and he always has been a little shy
of the 24, so you can imagine the condition of his nerves
after that experience. Here's an ironic top off to the whole
affair, almost funny but not quite. The movie booth was
playing records at the time George was telling us his story.
When he left us and he walked up the hill to the officer's
area, the record playing was "The Last Round-Up".

I guess it's time to sign off for tonight sweet. I'll see if I
can find time to write out at the line tomorrow, if there's no
work for we electricians.

I guess you know brown eyes that I love you terribly.
Those pictures sure done wonders to my morale. I'm
serious when I say you're wonderful and I've never been
more serious in my life as when I say – I love you. Good
night my darling, I miss you and I'll be seeing you.

Love forever,
Dick

Nose art of the B-24 "Double Trouble" that my
Grandpa flew in while in the Pacific.

Sept. 9, 1945

My Very Dearest Anna:

Sunday has rolled around again. Time's been going a little faster lately it seems. I hope it even goes faster until I'm with you.

I'm taking a little vacation from the line this morning. Most of the planes have flown down to Manila anyway so there wouldn't be any work to do. Capone and Steppe went this morning. I would have liked to go but they had a full load and there wasn't room.

I'll be working this afternoon though. I just volunteered for it. It's for a good cause otherwise you'd never catch me volunteering. They're building an enlisted men's club and we're anxious to get it done to have some sort of recreation facilities. The officer's have already built theirs and I have to give them credit, they did a swell job but we're out to build an even better club.

I sure wish they'd move that airstrip in another direction. Traffic's been heavy all morning. Every couple of minutes there's a plane taking off over our tent. A guy would be a nervous wreck if he lived at the end of an airstrip very long. Whoever picked out our camp location must have been deaf and dumb.

I heard another rumor today. The original was that 15 crews are going home. The latest is that the 6 oldest crews are going home. If they send them in groups of six, I'll only have to sweat till the third group leaves. No matter how they work it as long as they send us home by crews, I stand a chance of going home fairly soon. But if they decide to go by discharge points I'm stuck. I only have 40 or 45, and right now 85 is required. I'll have to quit for the time being sweet, but I'll finish this up this evening when I have more time.

I love you.

Back again honey, did you miss me? No, I don't suppose you did in this case. Then I'll ask do you miss me? 'Cause I certainly miss you darling, more than you know. I

220

just come from the show. I didn't stay long – no picture's good enough to sit through in the rain and it just started raining.

Darling, they had something strange for supper tonight. They called it ice cream, it was cold and fluffy with a vanilla flavor to it. You know I wouldn't be surprised if something like that won't become popular some day. No kidding we did have ice cream tonight, another point in favor of the ice machine. I'll admit it didn't compare with Goshen Dairy stuff but it sure tasted good after so long.

Before they go serving the pleasant added attractions though, I wish they'd do something about the main course. We haven't had fresh meat for over two weeks, all we get is canned stew and hash. I complained at Mindoro about pork two weeks solid, now I'd give anything for just one of those pork chops. I give the cooks here credit for once. With what little food they got to work with they do a good job on it, for a change. They used to be the laziest bunch of cooks to ever adorn a mess hall. With the coming of the ice age they seem to have acquired a little energy.

I just made a cup of coffee, have some? O.K. I admit it's not so good, but I know you can make a good cup of coffee for a midnight snack. Or rather a five o'clock A.M. snack. I'm so used to fixing something to eat before bedtime, I'm afraid I'll be spoiled. But I know you have the same habit so we won't disagree on eating, will we? We'll have the refrigerator stocked at all times.

I didn't hear from you today, but I did hear from Mom. She said Roy Belknap was here somewhere. I wish she'd give his address. She told me Earl Simmers was in the Philippines but didn't give me his address. I found out when I saw him, he was in the 90th B. Gp. a couple miles down the road from us. If Roy's here somewhere and I know his outfit, I can soon find him. The trouble is there's the 5th A. Force, the 7th, the 13th, the 8th, and I'll be darned if I can go around every one looking for him.

I don't believe that story about Barney either. Rumors like that start easily. I couldn't see Barney taking his own life. He wasn't that kind of guy.

Capone and Steppe must be going to stay at Manila for a while. They aren't back yet. Steppe is going to bring back some Manila whiskey so we can trade it for some plywood and planks to build our tent up. If our plans work out we'll really have a nice place to live. If we're here any length of time it's going to be cold and darned if I feel like freezing in an open tent. I hope if I do any shivering this winter it will be in New Phila.

Darling, it's getting late, so I'll sign off this time. I suppose you know brown eyes that I love you. If you don't, you'd better start believing it. I do love you Anna, maybe it won't be too long till I can look into those brown eyes and tell you in person. Good night, darling, I'll be seeing you.

Love forever,
Dick

Grandpa (right) in front of the Enlisted Men's club on Okinawa.

SIX LOCAL YOUTHS MEET IN MANILA

Six New Philadelphians, all in the armed forces in the Philippine war theatre, held a reunion recently at a Red Cross center near Manila, according to word received here today by former Mayor Arthur H. Williams of this city from his son-in-law, Pfc. Bob Black, who is with a U. S. Army Air Corps airdrome Squadron.

The group, which renewed old frendships, included Jack Bussinger, 144 Fourth street, SW.; Robert Haman, 740 Second street, NW.; Richard Moore, 140 Bank Lane, SW.; Art Agosti, 255 Ray avenue, NE., and Hank Crites.

According to Pf. Black, the six boys made arrangements for a second get-together meeting.

In February of 1945, the Allies had bombed the city of Manila to drive out the Japanese Army. During this time, the Japanese troops brutally executed men, women and children. The city was destroyed, 100,000 were killed, dubbing it the Manila Massacre.

I can only imagine what it was like for Grandpa to go there nearly 8 months later.

Sept. 24, 1945

My Very Dearest Anna:
Here I am again, after a short delay of a few days. I've been plenty busy the last few days up on the line, but from now on I may have more time. I got my job changed from the line to working in the P.X. I start my new job tomorrow and I should like it. Work starts at one in the afternoon and

224

there's not much work to it. And the best part, we have
Sunday off. If I discover some hidden bad point about the
job, I'll get sent back to the line. Oh yes, another good
point, the new job keeps me off of K.P. that's what
convinced me.

I suppose you notice this pen writing funny. I dropped it
again and spread the point a little more. I give it just one
more fall before I have to give it up.

This crew is beginning to take over the 530th. Capone is
now commanding officer of the squadron. I'm in the P.X.
department, Red Price is the chief ice man, Spencer's in
armament, and Avery is duty sergeant.

There is the big joke, Avery as duty sergeant. It's his
job to assign guys to K.P., details and guard duty and
believe me it's a job and a headache. Some guy is always
giving an excuse at the last minute why he shouldn't be on
detail and then you have to run all over the place finding
someone to take their place.

A guy just come to the tent and asked for Avery. We
said what's the matter, has he got you on K.P.? He said no,
he put a couple of cooks on the K.P. roster for tomorrow.
So you see, the duty sergeant has his trouble too. From now
on I won't hate the duty Sgt. I'll just pity him.

One of our boys is going home soon. Red Price has
enough points to go. Noonan was on the shipping list too.
They had men with 50 points on up but they took off all
guys with under 80. So Noonan stays with us for a while
longer. Here I am with a mere 45 points. I'm stuck for quite
a while, I'm afraid.

They've shipped quite a few guys from other groups in
here to await shipment home and now the place is crowded
as the devil, far too crowded. The meals at the mess hall get
worse by the day. We have hash, stew or spam every meal.
That's all we've had since we got here, no fresh meat
whatsoever. I'm getting tired of it, I no longer get any

225

enjoyment out of eating. I'll probably look like one of those German atrocity pictures if the meals don't improve soon.

I'm glad you added (in the Army) when you said I wouldn't escape K.P. After all I didn't expect you to put me on K.P. when we're married. Oh, I'm willing to help with the dishes all right, but I won't help with the cooking. I'll sit in my favorite easy chair, with my favorite slippers, reading my favorite newspaper, and when you have supper ready you call "Darling, supper's ready". It will be wonderful, I won't have to grab a mess kit and wait in line a half hour. Just walk up to the table, sit down and eat at leisure.

I guarantee your money would last over here. I did buy a leather jacket for $30 this month. The damn Army never would issue us one like they're supposed to and I've always wanted one. It has one of the pictures from the squadron painted on the back, it's pretty sharp. The picture is "Double Trouble" a silhouette of a woman sitting on a champagne glass that's where the Double Trouble comes in.

The other day I caught up on my work. I rode around the line in a jeep looking at the pictures on the planes. There are really some good ones, I'd like to have a camera and lots of film to take pictures of them.

There is "Deanna's Dreamboat" a pilot who used to know Deanna Durbin had her picture painted on the plane; "Superchick" a woman with nothing on but a Superman cape; "Lucky Strike", "Undecided", "Virgin Abroad", "Liberty Belle", "Dragon Lady", "Shittininnigitlin", "Bread Line in '49". There's really a variety with the emphasis on unclad females. There are some works of art on their planes. One of the best was named "Daisy Mae" with small letters "with a little persuasion". I think most of these Air Force men have their minds in the gutter when naming the airplane.

I guess it is a problem how Gene and Ethel's romance will come out. But I thought most people knew where we stand with one another. They should have a pretty good idea anyway. I know myself that there could be no one else for me. I love you so much Anna. I know each day that passes brings us closer to the day we'll be together, but dog-gone those days go awfully slow.

There's not much more to write about tonight darling. Maybe with my new job I'll have more time for writing.

I've told you hundreds of times, sweet, but do you mind if I keep telling you. I love you brown eyes, with all my heart. And I miss you more and more each day we're apart. Goodnight sweetheart, pleasant dreams and "I'll be seeing you".

Love always,
Dick

Some nose art on the aiplanes that Grandpa had described.

My Very Dearest Anna:

This has been a pretty nice Sunday. You know it does a guy good to have a day off once in a while. I think I found a pretty good deal in that P. X. job. We worked hard yesterday, cleaning up in the morning for inspection and inventory in the afternoon. But today I set aside for relaxation and catching up with my writing.

I didn't expect to do much relaxing though, there was supposed to be a typhoon hit last night with winds up to 60 m.p.h. Fortunately, it didn't hit us, there's quite a bit of wind right now but no rain with it. It seems as if every time they warn us of a typhoon coming, nothing happens. It's when the damned thing takes you by surprise that it really hits.

They called us all down to headquarters last night. They had us fill out a paper with our home address and if you wanted to remain in the Army upon return to the States. Whether that means we'll soon be returning to the States or not, I don't know, there are rumors to the effect that we will soon be heading home. Naturally, I don't put much faith in rumors. I do know I gave them an emphatic NO!! as to staying in the Army. (That damn wind is blowing the paper all around so excuse the blots).

I see you still don't understand the Air Corps. You see they only have about thirteen planes in the squadron and naturally the oldest crews got to fly them up here. The rest of us had to come by boat. I didn't mind too much, I enjoyed the boat ride for a change, but it's much too slow as a means of traveling. We were lucky to get to fly a plane over here. If we had went overseas last December it would have been by boat.

Be sure to let me know how Philly comes out with her football this year. I'd like to be home for the Thanksgiving game but that's quite a bit to hope for.

I thought I left my animal kingdom back at Mindoro but I had a surprise today when I opened my bag and found chewed up paper and cloth on top. Further investigating I found a rat's nest in the bottom of the bag. The big rat got away but there were about four little ones that we killed. They had holes chewed in most of my flying equipment. I'm glad they didn't choose the bag with my clothes.

I heard a rumor today that they're going to get fresh meat at the mess hall this week. I hope that rumor is true. They'd better get me home or get me some food or I'm going to lose a little weight.

I guess there's not much to write about sweet, so I'll sign off for today. Speaking of rumors I heard there's a guy on Okinawa by the name of Moore who is very much in love with a girl named Anna. Now there is one rumor that I know is true. Maybe because I'm the guy and you are the one I love so dog-gone much. You're wonderful brown eyes, you have no idea how much I miss you. I can't wait till I have you in my arms again and can tell you "I love you". Goodnight, darling and

Love Forever,

Dick

Oct. 2, 1945

My Very Dearest Anna,

I just got back from a tour of Okie Island. We were going to the P.X. warehouse to return some bottles and took a couple wrong roads there by seeing a little of the place. I'll admit there's not too much to see but it is a little better looking than most of the holes I've been stuck in

229

overseas. I thought I'd write before chow. I got a letter from you yesterday. I noticed it had been sent back for more postage. It looks as though the post office is getting rather C.S.

So you have fly trouble. That's one thing I can say never bothered me over here. Rats, mosquitoes and hundreds of other bugs but flies never give me any trouble. I think I'll have to put my mosquito netting on my bed again. Last night I was awake a couple hours scratching a couple mosquito bites. For some reason or other the species on this island seem to itch more than any others that have bitten me. Just so I don't get malaria from them I won't mind the bites so much.

The typhoon we were supposed to get never did go past a slight windy stage. I'm thankful for that, I can only stand being made homeless once, that was enough for me.

I suppose there will be quite a rush for the chow line today. The rumors about getting fresh meat were right. I'll certainly be glad to get off that stew and hash diet. It was getting so I felt like throwing up every time I looked at the trash they were serving. Just the other day I saw a dog eating out of the garbage can. I gave it a kick and said "Get the hell in the mess hall and eat, you're no better than us". (It's only a joke, but that's about the way the situation stands.)

I wish I were home so you wouldn't have to sit at home by yourself every time the family is away. I know how lonesome it is with nowhere to go and nothing to do. I get plenty of sleep lately, I guarantee that.

I see Dort is in a hurry for us to get married. She has her reasons anyway. I think they could send Mom and Dad to the movies. Harold has a car too so they have an advantage.

Double dates are all right once in a while but I like it better when we're all by ourselves. At least you don't have

230

Harold kidding you about your laugh. One thing though we had the car, but when I get a car of my own we won't have to worry about that.

That was quite a dream you had. Be sure and let me know how it comes out. I wonder how Toad West ever entered into it. It's natural for you to worry about your hair though. I used to dream about you and never get to talk to you in them but the last few we did quite a bit of talking.

We'll do plenty of bowling, if I get home in time, and I certainly expect to be before the bowling alleys close. Only I'm going to be very much out of practice, but you'll have to go some to beat me once I get started (Ahem, the old master is talking now). I promise not to beat you too badly though.

That job you have doesn't sound too good, especially the hours. That shift ruins the whole day what kind of work is it, seeing it's a bakery I'd think it wouldn't be very easy. There's no future in working too hard.

I don't have much more time for writing now honey so I'll sign off. As always, brown eyes, I love you. You don't know just how much. I'm in the mood for a good long boat ride as soon as possible. I can't wait to see you once again— no more good-byes this time. So long this time, I miss you darling and I'll be seeing you.

Love forever,

Dick

New York, Oct. 11 (INS)—Reports from Manila today said that a 12-hour typhoon had left 90,000 American soldiers homeless on Okinawa and killed at least five persons.

CBS Correspondent John Adams said that travelers from Okinawa reported that winds reached a peak of 120 miles an hour and that if the storm had occurred a month earlier it might have changed the whole pattern of our occupation.

No details were available on damage to naval installations, Adams said, but he quoted returned correspondents s saying that many small craft were seen beached on the shore.

Adams said that 500 army nurses were threatened when their tents and all personal belongings were swept away by the strong winds.

Okinawa Typhoon Junction

More complete reports placed the toll of last week's Okinawa typhoon at 28 dead, 70 missing, 91 seriously injured and 332 hurt. Three navy vessels were sunk, 30 were grounded and three others damaged.

The twister, which attained speeds of 130 miles an hour before recording instruments were blown away, made a shambles of the navy's advanced base, piled high with men and materiel for the previously planned Japanese invasion.

In response to a call from Gen. Joseph W. Stilwell, 10th Army commander, fleets of B-29s, C-54s and other aircraft flew in quantities of food and medicine. Other fleets of landing craft laden with rations and supplies sailed from the Philippines and near-by bases. They unloaded their cargoes directly on the beaches since all the island's piers and docks were wiped out by the big blow.

Newspaper articles from the typhoon that Grandpa had experienced in 1945.

Grandpa used to tell me a story about a typhoon that he had experienced in the Philippines. For two days they had to stay in the mess hall while the storm raged. The buildings at the camp were flimsy with tin roofs, and after the storm ended, they heard that one man that had been running for cover had been cut in half by a flying tin roof.

Nov. 15, 1945

My Very Dearest Anna,

It's a bit premature but today was Christmas for me. Yes, the Xmas box you sent arrived, darling, and it was really swell. It was in perfect condition too, all I can say is it was a rare occurrence in the annals of overseas package delivery for it to got here so quick and unscarred. Thanks a million sweet, as I said it was really swell, more than that it was wonderful. Tell your Mom the fellows in the tent and myself really enjoyed that fudge, it was delicious. I've asked everyone I know where I can find a camera, with no luck so far, but I'll get one, there's bound to be a 120 camera somewhere in camp. I just want to get it while I'm still here and get some pictures of life on Okie here.

The way rumors are now I think we'll be going up to Japan before long. They've consolidated all the squadrons into one and luckily it was the 530th they picked to use so I didn't have to move one inch for once. There are only low-pointers left now. I won't mind moving up to Japan now as long as I have to stay a while longer. My chances of getting home are better up there anyway. All of this B.S. about going home with the 380th B.G. as a unit was just B.S. If I go up to Japan and they let those battle stars loose I'll be on my way home in a hurry. I heard that they call this the "island of despair" back home because of the slowness in getting the men back home. But up in Japan they don't waste time getting them out. The last I heard Steppe was waiting for a boat, he's probably on his way right now.

I was working for a while this evening but took off early to get some letters written. The rush has died out over there anyway. Practically everyone has their beer. We've changed the P.X. hours back to 2 P.M. to 6 in the evening so that'll mean more time to myself. The P.X. will probably be closing any day. We have to turn in all the surplus stock before leaving. We no longer have movies, they turned in all the equipment yesterday. To see a movie now we have to go about a half mile down the road to another outfit and

233

I'm not that anxious unless some extra-special picture happens to be showing.

Since most of the fellows moved out of the tent, I haven't been going to breakfast anymore. It used to be a regular routine getting me out of the sack in the morning. I'd want to get up for breakfast, but that chilly morning air always made it awfully hard to crawl out of a warm sack. So after threatening to over turn the cot, to douse me with cold water, and finally pulling the blankets off me, they'd finally force me to get up. (Some of the names I'd call them during this early morning ritual weren't very nice). So now that all the early risers have left, leaving only myself and two others who love the sack more than I do, I now go hungry till dinner time. We'd better have a good heating system in our house or you'll have a rough time getting me out of bed on cold winter mornings. This morning took the cake though. Some Lt. woke me up this morning and asked if I had a pass to be in the tent. At first I thought he was kidding. It turned out he wasn't, they wanted every available man to help clean up the abandoned squadron area, and to be in the sack you had to have a pass proving you were on detail the night before. So I have the pass for tomorrow morning. I'm going to paint a "Do Not Disturb" sign and tack the pass on to it and sleep tomorrow morning.

They've been playing records over the loud speaker all evening. They're even playing Xmas carols already. "White Christmas", that's my theme song. White Xmas on Okinawa or Japan. It probably will be too, in fact, in Japan they have their winter issue of clothes. The way evenings are here we should get them too.

Since we don't have so many men anymore, the food situation has improved to perfection. It's as good now as any we ever got in the states. We've been having steaks, pork chops, beef and eggs, fresh potatoes.

By the way, don't get the idea I'm crazy, (maybe it's true), but this is another new pen I'm using. That makes a grand total of four. That other I bought wasn't very good and then we got some new ones at the P.X. I tried this one out and like the way it wrote so I bought it. Now I have in my possession a Parker, an Ink-o-Graph, a Wearever and now a Waterman, a pen for every occasion.

I guess I've about run out of news for now darling. Except for the same news I've been writing for almost two years now. Do you remember when I first started writing? It was a while before I got bold enough to say that I love you. One of these days I won't have to write it in a letter. I can tell you in person day after day. I do love you brown eyes, more than you can know. You're wonderful, sweetheart, and I miss you terribly. Just think one more month is half over, that day we've been looking forward to will come before we know it (I keep telling myself). Good night, sweet, I'll be thinking of you, I love you very much, I miss you and I'll be seein' you.

Love Forever and Always,

Dick

Grandpa (left) and his buddies on Okinawa.

Grandpa (third from left) and his buddies on Okinawa.

This is where my Grandpa's letters end (for the most part), and my Grandma's letters begin. I know he wasn't allowed to keep the letters that Grandma had sent him because he was limited in what he could carry. Those that he was able to keep were the few that he could carry and the ones that were "returned to writer", sent back to Grandma around the time that he was coming home. I'm not sure what happened to most of the letters that he was writing to her at the time and why they weren't saved.

CHAPTER 18
Letters from the Homefront

Miss Anna Wyatt
208 W. St. Clair Ave.
New Phila, Ohio

> *S/Sgt. Richard B. Moore*
> *ASN 35922674*
> *530th Bomb Sqdn.*
> *380th Bomb Grp.*
> *A.P.O. 337 c/o PM*
> *San Francisco, Calif.*
> (Okinawa)

November 19, 1945

My Very Darling Dick,
I just came home from doing some Christmas shopping.
I spent sixteen dollars and only have a couple presents to
show for it. Mom's birthday is a week from today and I
haven' gotten her anything yet. She won't give me any
suggestions so I'm really up against it. Not unless I buy her
a dress and then she'd have to pick it out, so that wouldn't
be any surprise. And she wants to be surprised!
It is raining today so I don't suppose we'll be very busy
at the bakery.
Aunt Ada and her family was down yesterday. My
cousin Lela is really growing up. I think she's a lot nicer

than she ever was. I can hardly wait for her to be eighteen or nineteen tho. Maybe when she is that age I can go to her house for a vacation. Right now she is a little young for me to run around with. There is quite a gap between 15 and 18 (well, almost 18).

Mary likes some boy from Dover but Dad won't let her go with him. He called up yesterday and wanted her to go to the show with him but Dad said she couldn't. The old meanie. His name is Gene Miller and I think he's very nice. Not a bit smart or ornery like most boys are today. Mom and I both don't see any harm in her going to the show with him once in a while, but Dad says she has to be 16 before she can go with boys and what he says goes. I ought to know. We could have been having lots of fun before you went to the Army but Dad wouldn't let me "date". You know, I'm surprised he even let me go with you when you came home on your first furlough. If he wouldn't have, tho, he never would have been able to live with me.

I saw George Reesman and Eleanor Pringle up town. I just wonder if they are engaged yet. He was home not so long ago, so I was surprised to see him. I thought they would get engaged as soon as he came home before but they didn't.

I finally got that reprint of the picture I said I would send you. I'll admit it's terrible of me but it's not bad of Mrs. Rafferty and Norma and they're the ones I want you to see. I wish Pauline could have been on the picture too, but since she was the one who snapped the picture that was impossible.

It is getting late so I better close and get ready for work.

As always, my darling, I love you very much. I love you like I've never loved anyone before. I think you're positively wonderful. I miss you more and more each day, if that is possible. I miss you so terribly now.

240

All my love always,
Anna

S. Sgt. Richard B. Moore
A.S.N. 35922674
530th Bomb Sqdn., 380th Bomb Gp.
A.P.O. 337 c/o P.M.
San Francisco, Calif.
(Okinawa)

Miss Anna Wyatt
208 St. Clair Ave. S.W.
New Philadelphia
Ohio

Nov. 24, 1945

My Very Dearest Anna:
Darlin', you have very little faith in me, please don't blame me for the postal service. And how about next time you don't hear from me for a week, don't get the idea I don't love you anymore. Anna, I'll love you forever and a day. This was my lucky day too, for I had the first letter from you in about six days, it was an extra-special letter too for it had the picture of you in it. It certainly is a swell picture too, this Moore is a lucky guy to have such a pretty girlfriend as you.
Honey, when you're letters get boring I'll let you know, and they never have been boring to me yet. If your letters are boring all I can say is that boredom is a wonderful feeling. I've told you before and I'll tell you again, over here, your letters are the only thing that makes life bearable. They mean the world to me darling, and why not, I love you so much.

It looks as though I'm leaving the scenic and beautiful island of Okinawa. You'd be surprised to hear where I'm going though. Not to Japan, but back to my old stomping grounds, Luzon, in the Philippines. It's not just rumor, it's fact unless they change the orders. I don't know just when we're leaving but it should be the next few days. It's to some replacement sqdn. of some kind. What will happen to us down there I don't know but I just hope we get our battle stars once we leave the 380th for then I'll be sitting on top of the world.

Don't worry, I've counted my points carefully and I still can't make over 45. If I had 50 it would at least be something to look forward to, I mean, I would know for sure I'd be going home real soon. There are still guys around here with over 80 points, but in my case, I don't know what the devil they'll do with me. I'm hoping for the best though.

The old P.X. is closed down now. They turned all the stock in that was left over. That puts me out of a job till I leave, so now for sure I should have time for writing. I think I'll sign off now darling and write again tomorrow.

As I said before, sweetheart, please don't doubt the fact that I love you. I do, brown eyes, and I always will. A girl as lovely and wonderful as you, well, I couldn't help but fall for you. I miss you Anna, it don't seem fair. The damned war is over, why don't they get us home. I want to be with you so much sweet, we certainly have a lot of wasted time to make up for. Goodnight honey, "I'll be seeing you" and I love you with all my heart.

Love forever,

Dick

On Dec. 1st, 1945, Grandpa left Okinawa in a C-46 Commando, a transport plane, landing at Clark Field on

Luzon. He then took a shuttle plane to Nielson Field and reported to 22nd Replacement Depot for reassignment to the 91st Replacement Battalion, changing his address to A.P.O. 714.

(Luzon)

December 2, 1945

My Very Darling Dick,
I still haven't heard from you. I don't know what to think, either, unless you are moving to Japan and haven't had time to write. Pauline said maybe you were flying home and would drop in any day now. Boy, but she's a dreamer. I've given up those kind of dreams long ago. They always end in disappointment.
I don't want to brag (much) but was I ever on the ball last night. Dort and I and the rest of my family went bowling and I beat them all. I started out my first game with three strikes and than a spare all in a row. I got another strike and a spare before the game was over so I ended up with a score of 168. I thought that was pretty good considering I only got around 70 the last time I bowled. Dort rolled a swell game, too. She got 155 her first game. I didn't do so well on my second game. I got 150 that

time. *And Dort got 105. I think the reason Dort didn't do so well the second game as she did her first was because the pin boy started to get "cute" the second game and it made her so mad she couldn't bowl right. Our pin boy, on the second ball, would set a pin in each gutter. Not that we were throwing gutter balls, because we weren't. (Well, not all the time, anyway) And when we'd get a strike he'd hurry up and stand up a pin and yell to us that we didn't get them all. He didn't bother me, but he did Dort and she was ready to skin him alive.*

I got your Christmas card yesterday. I mean I bought yours yesterday. I have it all ready to mail. I hope I'm sending it early enough. With Christmas coming and all I suppose it will take longer for a letter to come and go. The mail will be so rushed and over-burdened.

Mom and I went up to Massillon yesterday morning to see the new O'Neill shop that opened up Friday. Was that place ever packed, especially down in the basement where we each bought two towels and two pairs of pillowcases. Those are two items that are really scarce and probably will be for some time to come. I'm putting my towels and pillowcases away in my hope chest. Maybe when I get married they will be plentiful in the stores but just the same I'm not taking any chances. Then again they still might be plenty scarce.

With all these strikes going on I suppose it will be some time before peace time production is up to par again.

It's been a week now since Gene got home, and I've only seen him about twice. That's the way it goes. They are gone for years and when they finally do get home, I only see them once in an age. Like Raymond Griffey, I saw him a few times when he first got home but I haven't seen him since. They all seem to disappear.

I hope I hear from you tomorrow. I have to hear from you sometime, maybe tomorrow will be my lucky day. I love

you so very much, darling, I really feel blue when I don't
hear from you. I miss you so terribly, I can hardly wait till
you are home again.

Love always,
Anna

December 9, 1945

My Very Darling Dick,
    I don't have to go to work today so Dort and I are
going skating this afternoon. It's been so long since I've
skated I only hope I can stand up. I don't care for skating
so very much anymore but I might not have another chance
to go skating for a long time so I thought I'd go. The bakery
will be closed until Wednesday so that will give me a nice
vacation.
    I got a check in the mail yesterday from the
government. It was my civil service retirement. It only
amounted to fifteen dollars, but 15 dollars now is almost a
weeks' wages.
    I was sure glad to get that check. It's almost like having
15 dollars just gave to me for nothing. I'd been trying to
figure how I was going to be able to bank 25 dollars this
month and still buy all the Christmas presents I'd like to. I
wanted very much to get 300 dollars in the bank before the
first of the year and now I'll be able to. I couldn't be any
happier over that check if it had been for 50 dollars instead
of 15.
    We went bowling again last night but I didn't do near
so good this week as last. I only got 112, Dort got 90 and
Mom got 83. We only bowled the one game because Dort
and I had to be down at Pauline's by 9:30. Genie and Ethel
were there and we were going to play the mystic board. We
couldn't get it to work right, tho, so we gave up and played

245

five hundred rum the rest of the evening. Genie won but I ran him a close second until the last hand, then he got around hundred points and won the game with flying colors. Ethel was in the hole the whole game until the last couple hands. I think she ended up about 20 points to the good. "Babe" had his car or I suppose Ethel and Gene would have gone some place instead of spending a quiet evening at home. I like those quiet evenings at home. We'll have to invite Gene and Ethel down to my house some night to play cards after you get home. I bet we could have a lot of fun. I wish I could play cards like you can. You'll have to teach me some of the different kinds of card games like hearts. Please!

I had better close now and go help get dinner. I must admit this isn't much of a letter but at least you will know I am thinking of you. I think and dream of you all the time, darling. I love you so much and you're so wonderful. I can't keep you out of my mind.

Love forever,
Anna

I love you

When I was a kid and I would go to Grandma and Grandpa's house, we often played 500 rummy. It is one of my favorite memories of spending time with both of them. Grandma really loved playing that game.

December 11, 1945

My Very Darling Dick,
As far as I know I'm going skating tonight with Dort. She is supposed to come down after work and let me know if she is allowed to go or not. I sure hope so. We had so

much fun skating last Sunday afternoon. I've never had so much fun in ages. I don't expect to have as much fun tonight as I did Sunday but I still want to go.

I start to work tomorrow again. I was up the store for a while this afternoon helping to clean up. We dusted all the cans off, mopped the floor and washed the windows. It didn't take us long. Just long enough to get all dirty.

Mom and I actually started a Christmas saving fund this year. A dollar a week for 50 weeks. We've been meaning to for a couple years and never got to it. I don't know what happened before we knew it we were in the bank signing our names and giving the cashier our money. We also started one for Mary. We're each going to give $.25 a week and when December rolls around next year she will have $25 to spend for Christmas. Mom and I are going to try and not tell Mary we have this Christmas fund started for her so it will be a surprise to her when the check comes. She'll probably know it, tho, before this month is out. When it comes to things like this Mom and I can't keep a secret. I can keep a secret better than Mom can but that isn't saying much. She can't keep a secret hardly at all.

We wrapped all our Christmas presents yesterday afternoon. Maybe we were rushing things a bit but we wanted to get them wrapped and checked off our list. I still haven't bought Mom's present but I think I'll get her a housecoat I saw up at the Ideal Store. I never knew it could be so hard finding her a present. They're plenty of things she needs but I can't seem to be able to find any of them in the local stores. Boy, honey, are you lucky you don't have to worry about buying Christmas presents. They are sure one big headache.

Another week has gone by and I haven't heard from you. This is getting to be a habit. And a bad habit at that. It probably isn't your fault, tho, that I haven't heard from *you. This postal service is sure getting terrible. What do I mean, "getting". It has been terrible for a long time.*

I have to go clean-up darling, so I will close for now. There isn't much news lately to write about so I hope you will forgive some of these letters I have been writing. I love you so much, I have to write to you whether there is anything to write about or not, just to tell you how terribly much I do love you. I don't want you to ever forget that. And if I don't write, you might think I have forgotten you. And I don't want that to ever happen.

Love always,
Anna

Dec. 17, 1945

My Very Darling Dick,

Still no letter from you. It will be two weeks tomorrow since I last heard from you. If I didn't know better I'd be tempted to agree with Mom that you were on your way home, but the real reason is probably because you are being moved to Luzon. I suppose by now you are no longer on Okie, unless, of course, the Army changed its mind and didn't move you at all. Surely, tho, I'd have heard from you if you didn't get moved.

I have to go uptown this morning but it's so cold out and thought I'd leave for work early and do the little shopping I have to do then. That way I can save myself a trip in this awful cold. I have to go to the bank and deposit another dollar on my Christmas savings. And I also want to try and get Mom a pair of house slippers to match the blue striped jersey housecoat I got for her for Christmas. Since last week was a short week I only get ten dollars and with the ten dollars I did have that only gave me a mere 20 dollars to go shopping with up at Massillon. And after buying Mom's present, I only had a couple dollars left so you can see I'm pretty well broke. I don't care, tho. I have all my presents bought now and I won't have any need for money before pay day, except for those house slippers and I think I'll be able to afford them.

After living here for seven years without running hot water, at least we have it. Last Saturday afternoon, the plumbers came down and connected the gas heater and water tank. We had had the tank for a couple weeks but had difficulty in getting a heater. It sure is wonderful not having to heat water for every little thing.

Please excuse this writing. I'm breaking in this pen for Mom and it doesn't seem to want to write so smooth. The point is too fine to suit me.

The boys who were supposed to leave for the Army this Friday won't have to go until after Christmas. The draft board is sure getting big-hearted. I wish it could have been big-hearted a couple years ago at this time. I thought it was awful making you go into the Army right before Christmas. (I thought it was awful making you go into the Army, period).

We started on Christmas house cleaning today. We washed down the kitchen and now my hands are so rough. They're even worse than dish-pan hands.

I had better be closing my darling. This darn pen is making me so mad. It almost refuses to write at all now. So before I lose my temper and break it into a thousand pieces I will close.

Take care of yourself, darling, and don't forget I love you more and more. I hope and pray I hear from you soon. I'm getting so discouraged. Every day I get up with the thought "well, maybe I'll get a letter today". And I always feel pretty good until the mailman comes. Then when he only leaves a couple Christmas cards, I don't feel so good.

In fact, I feel pretty darn blue. I love you so terribly much darling, I'd give anything for a letter from you.

All my love always,
Anna

530th BOMBARDMENT SQUADRON (H) AAF
380th BOMBARDMENT GROUP (H) AAF
APO 925

2 January 1945

_C_E_R_T_I_F_I_C_A_T_E_

This is to certify that S/Sgt Richard B. Moore ASN 35922674, flew Combat Missions over Balikpapan, Island of Borneo, 4 June 1945, 24 June 1945, 28 June 1945.

S/Sgt Moore has a total of 59:00 Combat Mission time.

William D. Brew
WILLIAM D. BREW
2nd Lt., Air Corps
Commanding

(Luzon)

My Dearest Darling,
  I just got back from Penny's where they had sheets on sale. Mom and I had to wait in line forty minutes to get one sheet. That's all they would allow us. Mom doesn't need sheets but I wanted them for my hope chest. Sheets are scarce these days and when ever any store gets them there is always a rush to get them. Maybe, by the time I need sheets they will be on the market but than again they may not, so I'm not taking any chances.
  I also bought a luncheon set today. It has to be embroidered and it looks like a lot of work. It will be worth it tho. It should be beautiful after it is finished. I'm working on a pair of pillowcases now. I'm going to have to hurry up and finish them so I can start on the luncheon set. I've been on them for so long now, I don't dare let them go until last. They never would get finished then.
  I got the pictures your mom and dad took on my film but I don't know whether to send them to you, yet, or not. I thought, maybe, I'd wait until you got your permanent address, although, that may not be for some time. I could send them now and if you got them that would be swell. If you didn't, I could always have reprints made and send them to you later. I'll wait a couple days until I hear from you again and if you still have the same address I'll send them. And if you have a new one, well, I'll still send them. I have a picture here of Mary and I together but I can't make up my mind whether to send it or not. You have so many pictures of me now. I'm anxious to get those pictures you had taken on Okie. Surely you must have sent them by now. I had to iron yesterday morning so I didn't get a chance to write. And, anymore, I've been too tired to do anything when I get home after work.

251

I have to get ready for work. It's almost one and I haven't ate yet. I don't think I will tho. I had a glass of milk and a roll when I got home from Dover that should last me until supper. I can always eat a cookie if I get hungry before then. That's one advantage of working at a bake shop.

So long for now, my darling. I'm sorry this is so short but I really must hurry. I just want you to know I love you very very much. I hope I hear from you soon. I haven't heard from you yet this year.

Love always,
Anna

CHAPTER 19
Stateside Bound

On Jan. 14th, 1946, Grandpa went to Manila where he boarded a train heading to Clark Field. He stayed there at the 13th Air Force transient camp. Two days later, on Jan. 16th, he loaded up trucks for a trip to Fort McKinley near Manila.

After arriving there, he was assigned to the XIII Fighter Command, with the A.P.O. 719-1. On Jan. 24th, he reported back to the 22nd Replacement Depot for return to the United States. He was then assigned to the 266th Replacement Company, with the A.P.O. 714.

On Jan. 29th, 1946, Grandpa finally started his journey home to his Anna, when he boarded the U.S.S. John Land A.P.A 167. He left the Manila Harbor around noon, where he was undoubtedly happy because he was stateside bound.

(Aboard U.S.S. John Land)

January 29, 1946
I love you

My Very Darling Dick,
It will soon be two weeks since I last heard from you.
I'm hoping and praying that it means you are on your way
home. But I just know that eventually a letter will get here
and you will still be over there. The paper said there has
been a great slow-up in the delivery of mail. It said
something about there not being enough airplanes so the
majority of air mail is going by boat, taking as much longer
as 30 days to reach it's destination.
I hope, my darling, that by this time you have gotten
some mail. Surely you must have. Bill Erwin got home last
week. And last Saturday night when I was up at the Seabee
with Mom and Dad I noticed a lot more of the guys we
know are home. Tony Dergel, Joe Pompey, just to name a
couple.
You know where the Seabee is, don't you? It's where
Jackson's used to be. It seems to be a pretty nice place. At
least, what I seen of it. They have a room for "couples
only" and that's where we sat. They have a place to dance
if you want to or you can just sit and eat. They made very

*good hamburgers. The "Seabee" is another place we'll
have to go. I know it's a beer joint to some people but we
don't consider it that. And as long as Mom and Dad
approves of it, I guess there's no harm in being seen there.
I saw Mr. and Mrs. Davy leaving as we came in. I suppose
I would have recognized a lot of other people we know
except my glasses were steamed up and I couldn't see so
well.*

*Johnny Curran and Jean Willis got married last Sunday
afternoon. I had to work but I went to the wedding during
my lunch hour. It was a very nice wedding. It was a church
wedding but Jean didn't wear a gown. She wore a street
length gown but she still marched down the aisle. Tommy
and Bill Lan were ushers and "Buss" was best man. Buss
looked more scared than the groom. In fact, John wasn't
nervous at all. I know I will be tho, when I get married. My
throat will probably be so dry I'll never even be able to say
"I do", let alone repeat all those other things after the
preacher. But I'll cross that bridge when I get to it and in
the mean time I won't get any gray hairs worrying about it.*

*We have a big ironing to do today and I better be
getting to it. One-thirty rolls around pretty fast.*

*Dort said that Buehler's might need another girl at
their pastry counter. And she has been sort of
recommending me. I wish I could get a job there. It would
be all day work and as soon as you come home that's the
kind of a job I'll be looking for. And since Dort plans on
working there herself when she graduates, we'd be working
together. That would be swell!*

*I had better get started on that ironing, darling, so I
will close for now. Remember, honey, I love you with all my
heart and I'm still waiting. I promised I'd wait and I am.
Darling, you're worth waiting for. You're the most
wonderful guy I know or ever hope to know. Gee, but I miss
you so terribly much. Will that day when we're together*

255

ever come? As surely as the sun comes up in the morning, we will be together some day. Only I wish that day would hurry up and get here.

I love you.

Love always,

Anna

P.S. The mailman just came and brought a letter from you. I could kiss him for that. It's a wonderful letter and it had made me very happy. I'll answer it as soon as I can.

I love you,

Anna

January 30, 1946

My Very Darling Dick,

Am I ever an old sleepy head! I never got up until nearly ten o'clock this morning. That's really the latest I've slept for a long time. I'm going to have to see that it doesn't happen again. I usually wake up every morning at five till nine. It's uncanny how I would wake up at the same time all the time. Something went wrong this morning, tho.

I was so glad to hear from you yesterday, darling. It was a red-letter day for me so you see you aren't the only one who has red-letter days. Every day that I hear from you is a red-letter day to me. Too bad I don't have those red-letter days a little oftener, but when I do have them they sure are wonderful.

Yes, hon, Gene's a civilian all right. I haven't seen him for so long, tho, he might just as well be still in France. When he was there, at least I got a letter once in a while. Now I hardly know he exists. Darling you weren't <u>really</u> serious about him giving me a kiss for you, were you? I don't mind waiting for a <u>real</u> kiss from you.

256

I just saw your mom going down to the store so I went out a couple minutes to talk about our favorite subject – you. She feels the way I should feel (but don't). Not to expect you till we see you, although, I must admit I'm rather inclined to look at the bright side. I figure that, maybe, by some miracle, you will get home in February. If praying helps, you will. I miss you so much. They just can't keep you over there forever, although, they're sure trying.

Gee, darling, I was glad to hear nothing has changed between us. It had been so long since you had mentioned anything about the future that frankly I was worried. I love you so much, I'd simply die if you had changed towards me. I have so many things planned for us to do when you get home.

I guess I was wrong about Harold getting a discharge. He only has a 30 day leave which is up the 10th of February. It didn't take him a month to get home like he figured it would. Don't be surprised if you have him for a brother-in-law some day. I think Dort and him have had a date just about every night. It's going to be pretty hard on Dort when he goes back this time. They have had a chance to get acquainted this time.

I hate to close but I guess I'll have to. This is all the paper I have. I even got this last sheet out of the scrap pile. I'll write again soon, tho. In the mean time, remember, darling, I love you now and always will. "I'll be seeing you".

Love always,
Anna

January 31, 1946

My Very Darling Dick,

I just got home from town. Today is Dort's birthday so I went up and got her a present. It's colder out than I thought and I about froze. The wind is blowing so awfully hard that's probably what makes it so cold. Or, at least, it helps. While we were up town Mom and I stopped in at Grant's and bought a couple of Turkish towels. She got two for herself and I bought two for my hope chest. This will make me 13 towels in my chest. I don't think that's so bad considering towels are very scarce and hard to buy. I'm very proud of them, too. Mom is crocheting me a rug for my future bedroom. She's making it out of blue and pink yarn. Is it ever going to be beautiful! Effie Willis showed her how to make it. Effie made one for Jean and when Mom saw it she knew I'd want one so she looked all over for yarn. She couldn't find any when she first looked but Grant's got some in the other day so she hurried up and bought some. I think she is so wonderful to be making me a rug. She does so many things for me, I wish I could do some things for her.

While we were over to Dover this morning we stopped in at Cussins and Fern to see one new stove. We're to get it Saturday but we were anxious to see it so we went over and took a look. It's a gas range and it's not very big. Not near as big as our other one. We decided to get it all of a sudden. We hadn't planned on buying a new stove at all. We're getting a new cabinet sink, too, as soon as they come in. That's one thing we have planned on, tho. We need one pretty bad. We need a lot of things pretty bad to tell the truth. This house could do with a lot of new things and fixtures.

Well, my darling, tomorrow is the first of February. Another month is over. I hope and pray that we don't have to be separated very many more months. Maybe, February is our lucky month. Let's hope so.

If the points have been lowered to 45, then you don't have to wait for those battle stars. Or in the S. Pacific is the number of points needed 48? I thought, tho, they were lowered to 45 both in Europe and the S. Pacific. Boy, they better had be. In that case that means you'll be pretty sure to be home, at least, by April 30th. Right now, tho, that seems a long way off, too.

It's getting late, darling, so I'll bring this to a close for this time.

There's not much use in telling you that I love you, I've told you so many times now, but I think I will, anyway. And I'm going to keep on telling you I love you for the rest of my life, cause, darling, I do love you with all my heart.

Love and kisses,
Anna

February 5th, 1946

My Very Darling Dick,

You should just see me. I'm all up in pin-curls and if I don't look like something out of one of the Frankenstein's pictures. Well, maybe, I don't look quite that bad. At least, I hope not. I just got through washing my hair so I put it up for the night. Since I got my permanent a couple of months ago I haven't had to put up my hair, only when I wash it. I suppose, tho, by the time you get home I will once again have to go through all the misery and trouble of putting this stuff I call hair up every night. I just dread the thought but I do have some comfort in knowing I'm not the only girl in the world who has to put up their hair.

It has been raining all day, but still it is lovely out. Just perfect for a walk in the rain. Shall we go? Okay. Wait till I slip something on.

This isn't much of anything, darling, but at least you will know I'm thinking of you. Darling, I miss you so very much. I'm always thinking and dreaming of you. I love you more and more, Dick.

Love always,
Anna

CHAPTER 20
Coming Home

On Feb. 16th, 1946, Grandpa finally docked in the Frisco Harbor around noon after 19 days at sea. He debarked and loaded a ferry for a four hour trip to Camp Stoneman in Pittsburgh, California. He left there on Feb. 18th, and four days later, he arrived at Camp Atterbury in Indiana for processing to be discharged from the Army.

He was officially discharged on February 25, 1946, and by the 26th he had arrived home in NewPhiladelphia and into Grandma's arms. He was officially a civilian once again. And most importantly, after two years of waiting, he finally returned home to the most important thing in the world to him, his Anna.

☆ United States Navy ☆

KNOW ALL YE LANDLUBBERS by these presents that __RICHARD___ _L.MORRE___
(NAME AND RANK/RATE)
__380 T'S_ J O.V R_G.P.__
(UNIT TO WHICH ATTACHED)

crossed the high seas, homeward bound, aboard

U. S. S. _____JOHN L._____
Wherefore, he is duly described as an honorary member of the ship's company, and a charter member of the

Order of The Magic Carpet

WITNESS __E. M. ELLER__
James Forrestal
SECRETARY OF THE NAVY.   DATE __16 FEB 1946__   Captain, U.S. Navy.
18—46567-1   GPO

Grandpa's Navy Pass for his trip to the Frisco Harbor.

To you who answered the call of your country and served in its Armed Forces to bring about the total defeat of the enemy, I extend the heartfelt thanks of a grateful Nation. As one of the Nation's finest, you undertook the most severe task one can be called upon to perform. Because you demonstrated the fortitude, resourcefulness and calm judgment necessary to carry out that task, we now look to you for leadership and example in further exalting our country in peace.

Harry Truman

THE WHITE HOUSE

Upon returning home, he asked Grandma if he would marry her. Her response, "There's no sense in wasting all those wonderful letters!"

Four months later, on the Sunday afternoon of May 26th, 1946, Grandpa and Grandma were married at the Latter Day Saints Church on the South side of New Philadelphia. Dorothy was Grandma's Maid of Honor and Gene was Grandpa's Best Man. A reception was held at Grandma's house following the ceremony. After all that time of waiting and writing to each other, they were finally starting the life together that they had been dreaming of.

Grandpa and Grandma's wedding photo.

I know how the story ends, and it's a happy one. They go on to live a wonderful life together and have two kids, who gave them eight grandchildren who then brought them an incredible amount of great grand children, with the count still growing. Their love was handed down to all of us, making us better people than we could have dreamed to be. Their huge hearts and wonderful outlook on life created an amazing family. I could only dream to find a love as great as theirs and a person as lovely to share it with.

EPILOGUE

Just four days before their 49th wedding anniversary, Grandma passed away on May 22nd, 1995. Grandpa had stayed up with her all through the previous night talking about their lives together and all they had been through, not knowing that by the morning she would be gone.

Grandpa spent the next twelve years without her until he was killed in a car accident on August 6th, 2007, 62 years to the day that the Enola Gay dropped the atomic bomb on Hiroshima. On the morning of August 6th, 1945, Grandpa had woken up to find out that his mission was cancelled. During their briefing for that mission they were told there would be about 500 anti-aircraft guns pointed at them at one time. He always said that he probably wouldn't be here if it weren't for that plane, and neither would the rest of my family.

While I was close to Grandma for the 15 years of my life that I had the wonderful luck of knowing her, I knew my Grandpa for 27 years. He was my best friend. I spent the majority of my time with him through those years. Whenever I finished the day of classes throughout grade school and high school, it was a rush to get to his house so I could spend as much time with him as possible before I had to go home for the evening or to whatever sports practice I happened to be doing at the time. During college summer breaks or weekends I came home, I would spend it at

267

Grandpa's house all day until Mom got home from work, then it was time to hang out with her. I would have my friends meet me at Grandpa's or I would bring my friends along to visit. Often, a high school friend and I would rollerblade to his house to visit over Dixie cups of Mountain Dew, a Grandpa staple.

My sisters and I often used to joke with him about who his favorite granddaughter was. Always saying, "Of course, I'm Grandpa's favorite", to the response of "No, I am". And he would laugh, and say "you're all my favorites". Surprisingly, none of us really liked that answer. Each of us wanted to be the special one.

I've never known anyone like Grandpa and Grandma. Grandpa was my best friend and he was my favorite. I can't express in words how much I loved the both of them. My heart breaks when I think about the days that we lost them. Even as my heart continues to heal with every passing day, it will never be whole again. I miss them both very much, and can only hope that this book helps spread their story that I love so well and that their memories continue to live on. As I know they are both happy together somewhere, I still selfishly wish they were still here with me. Grandpa always said I was his pretty girl and he was my best friend, and they both were my home.

My only comfort is in knowing that wherever they are, wherever you go, I know they are together again and happy. And that is all Grandpa ever really truly wanted.

AFTERWORD

   While I was reading these letters, there were things that I recognized from my talks with Grandpa and from his belongings. Like a piece of jewelry, a photo, or even a story I had been told. When I read about his Air Corps photo being taken for the newspaper, I turned around and I could see the framed photo he was talking about sitting behind me on a shelf. Or I knew exactly where the bracelet was that he bought for my Grandma in the Philippines. It's now in my own jewelry box.

   After reading all of their letters, I have learned so much about the holes in the stories that my Grandpa would tell me. When I would come across a story I had heard before, it was as though I was apart of it. Since I knew about it already through Grandpa's stories, even though these stories had happened so many years before I even existed.

   I wanted to put this book together to preserve this piece of history. I wanted to tell their story so that more people than just myself could enjoy and remember who they were. The most important reason that I have put all of this together is that I never wanted to forget these details that made them who they were, as I already feel the accuracy of my memories slipping away. Muddled by the passing of time and the aging of the brain. I know that they will never be forgotten and that they will live on in our hearts and in our family legacy. I didn't want to lose this important piece of our family history, that was only a small story that took place during a big part of world history.

I started reading these letters so I could organize and copy them to share with my whole family since I know they feel as passionately about my Grandparents and their story as I do. I had this box of letters for years, never reading them, afraid of what they would hold. Afraid that it would be my very last time, in a way, to talk to Grandpa again. I will probably never learn anything new about their story. After my own journey of reading and researching, I'm really happy that I decided to open that box.

Continue the story of *My Very Dearest Anna* at
<u>www.dearestanna.com</u>

Featuring more photos, documents, and family
stories.

ABOUT THE AUTHOR

Kara Martinelli works in the television and film industry, mainly producing aviation documentaries, telling stories of veterans and airplanes. She currently resides in Ohio. This is her first book, which was written for her family.